LIVE LIKE A MILLIONAIRE ON $17,000 A YEAR

Lewis Harrison

Live Like a Millionaire on $17,000 a Year

www.lewisthinkandgrowrich.com

Illustration concepts by Dejan Ilijic, artwork by Kristina Tosic
Layout, design & cover by Blooming Twig Books LLC
www.bloomingtwigbooks.com

First edition 2008
ISBN 978-1-933918-38-9

DEDICATED TO

... all those honest, kind and committed people who work hard enough at their jobs to keep from getting fired and get paid just enough to keep them from quitting.

ACKNOWLEDGMENTS

Thank you to Bill Zanker, Harry Javar and the staff at the Learning Annex, Drew and John at Phimedia, Jeff Wolf and Paul Goldner for letting me see wealth up-close. Marc Becker for being there at the beginning and supporting me through the years, Iggy at the Golden Sands Resort and Spa in Malta for opening the 5-Star Chapter of my life and Zali Segal for teaching me the ins and outs of both barter and influence.

PREFACE

I'm writing this from a Five Star Hotel on the Island of Malta; I'm standing on the third floor terrace, looking out over the Mediterranean Sea. The television is on European Sky-Vision, tuned to a television show about San Tropez and the lifestyles of the rich who stay there, the announcer describing a lush high-end experience... It is almost an exact description of my lifestyle here on Malta. The cost for San Tropez? $1,200 a night. The cost for my trip? $350 for the week.

This is exactly what this book is about - Living Like a Millionaire on $17,000 a Year.

$$$

My journey to this lifestyle began about fifteen years ago when I agreed to accept a plane ticket and vacation package to Hawaii as payment for services I had provided to a client who, though experiencing a cash crunch, owned a time share in Hawaii and a powerful contact at one of the major airlines. I was willing to do this because they had what I needed at the time, and I wanted to continue serving their needs through my expertise as a consultant, coach, trainer and speaker on aspects of peak performance. Without the trading (i.e. barter) option they just would not have been able to afford my services.

Over time my skill in trading goods and services for other people's goods and services expanded to the point that I was creating more income by trading this for that than I was producing in cash income.

Somehow, over the years, I began to live like a millionaire on a middle class, working person's cash income. I had combined my street smarts, common sense, my father's entrepreneurial influence, quality mentoring and coaching from my wealthy friends, with my own intuitions. Through the synergy of these various factors I realized that I had found the Holy Grail, the secret code to living well. I organized my understanding of this secret code into a written text known as the Harrison Process for Self Actualization, which covers a lot of territory: wisdom, relationships, peak performance, wealth and more. It also, for the first time, addressed the issue of living like a millionaire without cash. The book you now hold in your hands is constructed of principles from The Harrison Process, and designed to help you live like a millionaire on $17,000 a year.

$$$

INTRODUCTION

What's the secret to getting rich? In the past it might have been organizational rank, hereditary titles, or social position that was the quickest path to wealth and power. Thankfully this is no longer the case. Today a highly creative person with access to information, ideas, and influence can transcend anything that could have been done in the past.

The greater your creativity, the greater your ability to change knowledge into information - information into measurable value - measurable value that can be converted to freedom, happiness and the things that wealth provides. This is a unique type of wealth that is created without the accumulation of cash.

$$$

The goal of the $17,000 dollar method, if studied and applied carefully, will be to show you how to live very well, with very little cash.

I have divided the information in this book into 15 sections, each one addressing the issue of how to get what you want and need with little or no money. How little? If every piece of information in this book is applied with clarity, conservation, balance, and wisdom, you will have all you need to live like a millionaire on $17,000 a year.

$$$

"Are you insane?" You might ask...

"No!" is my response.

"Out of the box?"

"Yes..."

"Unconventional?"

"Yes!"

"A little thrifty?"

"Yes!"

"Crazy?"

Not a prayer.

The entire program is based on the practical fact that I can convert \$1 of cash to about \$59 worth of goods and services. I can do this through the maximum utilization of ten key resources that are described throughout the book. These resources includes among other factors, the value of time, influence, information, and clarity of thought. I call these ten key resources Cashless Currencies because they bypass the need for cash in many, if not most, transactions.

Basic common sense tells us that everything has a cost. Unfortunately, the assumption that many of us make is that this cost will usually be in cash. Thus, we think we are limited in getting what we want or need, because we don't have enough cash.

This book will show you how to bypass cash as the primary tool for buying what you need and to increase the buying power of the cash you have.

There are five components to the \$17,000 system.

1. Change your way of thinking about money.
2. Observe the lifestyles of the rich and famous.
3. Greatly reduce your expenses.
4. Greatly increase the buying power of your cash.
5. Eliminate obstacles to your financial freedom.

Then, make wise choices once you have mastered steps 1-5.

Sections 1-6 are designed to change your way of thinking about money and introduce you to the lifestyles and living habits of the rich and famous.

Sections 7-12 are focused on reducing your expenses while increasing your income.

Sections 13-14 are concerned with traveling well with thrift.

Section 15 focuses on self-assessment and a transformation in thinking.

All sections in this book are essential reading if you are interested in living your best life with joy, and passion. However all of them require some thought and hard work in order to apply the information. No offense, but if you are interested only in getting stuff cheap, I recommend that you start at section 7 and end at section 14. Either way, I guarantee that you will learn much from my $17,000 method and greatly improve your quality of life.

Creating and sustaining wealth requires intelligence, common sense, intention, and a systematic approach for merging all of these. As mentioned in Section 1, there are many more millionaires now than ever before. This new wealth is largely due to measured planning and active re-investment of cash income. Just imagine the potential! You can do exactly the same thing, but with much more than just cash! Follow the guidelines and apply the tips presented in Live Like a Millionaire on $17,000 Dollars a Year and the sky is the limit.

You will live rich. I don't mean having nice vacation now and then. I mean traveling the world's capitals six months out of the year.

$$$

TABLE OF CONTENTS

IV. *The Alchemy of Wealth*

V. *The Obstacles and Bottlenecks*

VI. *From Obstacles to Assets*

VII. *Spend Less Cash to Survive*

VIII. *Spend Less Cash to Live Well*

IX. *Spend No Cash*

XV. *The Total Transformation to Wealth*

I. THINK LIKE A MILLIONAIRE

What Millionaires Have Told Me

Never assume that you know how a wealthy person thinks unless you are one. I have spoken to dozens of very wealthy people and have been surprised, shocked and amused at some of things they have told me. Usually I have met them at art shows, gallery openings, in the VIP areas of airports, at charitable events and through ordinary networking and socializing.

It was at a dinner party at a Billionaire's apartment in the Olympic Towers in NYC when I learned that he kept his indoor swimming pool – the one in his apartment - empty most of the time. "Why waste money to keep it filled with water when I'm seldom around to use it - even if it only costs a few thousand dollars a month," he told me.

I learned from the heir to one of the European Thrones that if you have influence, people will give you lots of interesting stuff for free, even if you haven't asked for it. I guess it's good to be close to the guy who would have been king if there was still a throne.

And I learned from a close friend, a man rich enough to buy countries, that it is wise to save your money for those things that are an expression of your passions. He brown bags his lunch, drives a ten year old Mercedes Benz, but will fly to Europe for a weekend to get in some great skiing.

I heard an interview with Donald Trump in 2007 and two things he said stuck in my mind. He takes home Doggie Bags and he's never used an ATM.

$$$

Some millionaires are psychologically secure, generous with others and content with their lives. They live out their passions and know how to go with the flow. Others worry about losing control and live under constant stress.

The most effective millionaires make decisions based on a combination of information, influence, ethics, vision, intuition and service. Those that seem to be less content make choices based on a type of greed that is detached from creating any benefit to those around them. They may like their chosen career, but it is still the application of power and wealth that motivates them. There is a type of narcissism that drives them and a certain level of effort that is required in order for them to stay balanced in life while maintaining control. Without a hyper sense of balance and clarity of purpose they end up the victims of greed, envy, ethical lapses, federal investigations, public disdain, multiple high priced divorces and a quality of life that in the end is a mile wide but only an inch deep. Worst of all they often end up dissatisfied with the life they have chosen. Clearly, trying to control everything is not the easiest path to wealth and happiness.

One millionaire I spoke with - a person of great clarity and depth - described the path to wealth and happiness in the following way:

It is as if you are on a surfboard in the ocean, looking at the shore. The wave comes; you cannot control the wave. What you can do is keep your balance on the board and surrender to the wave. You are surrendering to the wave but you are not resigned to it. There is a difference! If you just drifted in the ocean and let the wave throw you about until you landed on the shore you would probably land on your head, experience pain, discomfort and struggle. This is the end result of 'resignation'. Resignation is not the same as surrender.

He pointed out that when you surrender, you have the wisdom to control what you can and leave alone what you cannot. In life, to be happy, whatever our financial state, we must ultimately surrender to the wave of our passions. In fact, there is wisdom in knowing that the actualization of your passions will enable you to leave the world a better place than you found it. True wealth, even financial wealth is in part learning to surf on the wave of your passions, brought to you by nature, some divine essence... maybe God. In the end, you still must defend yourself from all the predators and victims in the world that will take advantage of your wealth and your generosity, but in the end you get to live very well, maybe even a life of great wealth and elegance if that is what you wish. And in the end, your wealth will lead to good will and a better life for others, whether your employees or your greater community, through the charitable acts you bring to the world at large.

$$$

The most important lesson I have learned from speaking and spending time with those of great wealth is that thinking about what it is to be a millionaire is not the same as thinking like a millionaire.

The Desire for Pseudo-Peak Experience: The Path to Poverty

The desire to be cash rich; to experience great wealth, is often connected to an individual's desire for peak experience. A peak experience is a moment, lasting from a few seconds to minutes, during which we feel the highest levels of joy, harmony, happiness, motivation, inspiration, and a sense of personal-actualization. The term "peak experience" itself is generally attributed to the psychologist Abraham Maslow, who originally discussed the concept in his 1943 paper A Theory of Human Motivation and wrote extensively on the subject in the mid-twentieth century.

Maslow studied healthy people, people who had the "full use and exploitation of talents, capacities, potentialities, etc." He was interested in Self-actualization: the attainment of the basic physiological needs of safety/security, love/belongingness, and self-esteem.

Maslow understood well the concept of peak experience: the realistic and full experience of value, individuality, consciousness, purpose, ethics and the higher reaches of human nature. People who have experienced peak experience have a more efficient perception of reality; they have comfortable relations with it. This can be extended into all areas of life. Those who have gone through peak experience are unthreatened and unfrightened by the unknown. They have a superior ability to reason and to see the truth in everything. They are logical and efficient.

Sadly, the term peak experience is commonly misused in popular culture to describe what is actually more of a pseudo peak experience; a pleasurable experience that makes you rethink the way you look at the world, i.e. a sunset, a vigorous mountain climb, or a particularly good conversation. A true peak experience isn't just temporary, but pervades all consequent thoughts and actions. The writer Colin Wilson points out that humans can't comprehend how often their own "sense of defeat" stops them from doing things that they probably could do well, and he points out that peak experience is able to show people that their power is far greater than they had ever imagined.

To live very, very well you must combine frugality while distinguishing between peak experiences and pseudo peak experiences. You must make choices that provide a route to personal growth, fulfillment, and a sense of personal power - all key elements to living rich on very little cash. The key is to work from a system that you can apply to create and sustain your own peak experiences.

$$$

How do Millionaires Think?

Millionaire thinking requires a sense of passion and a desire to share that passion. The money comes next, and when it does come, millionaires recognize the financial opportunities and act on them. They also recognize obstacles to wealth and avoid or transcend them.

Here are some of the dos and don'ts I have learned about how healthy, balanced and content millionaires think, and what they think about:

- Millionaires appreciate the wealth they have and the positive things it represents.
- They put aside quality time to enjoy their hobbies and passions, as well as the love of their family and friends.
- They are always on the lookout for and know how to find "good deals." Thus they are generally frugal and thrifty unless they are investing in something with a great return on investment or are investing in their passion.
- They avoid buying things just to impress others or to feed their insecurities.
- They give back: Charity and community service are key elements of living well. The truly rich know that the more they give the more they get.
- They generally did not plan on being millionaires. They acted on a passion and wealth was the end result, the gravy.
- They do not buy lottery tickets. They'd rather invest the dollar.

- They know how to sustain and expand whatever they have acquired.
- They understand that there are no free rides and there is no free lunch in life, so they don't waste time looking for them.
- They never define their wealth by cash alone.
- They keep track of where their money goes so they can make more of it.
- They never pay retail if they don't have to.
- They don't lick their own stamps. In other words, they hire someone to do it for them who is willing to do it for less then their own time is worth.
- They attract wealth through creative visualization and affirmations.
- They are informed consumers.
- They commit random acts of kindness.
- They ask for what they want and negotiate for better deals whenever possible.
- They buy low and sell high.
- They trade and barter whenever possible.
- They create wealth through self-assessment.
- They de-mystify financial concepts and understand how money is made and lost.
- They avoid impulse buys.
- They measure the growth of their wealth and have a general knowledge of how much cash they really have.
- They actively reinvest.
- They know how to budget their resources.
- They pay down their debts.
- They have an organized system for tracking their debts.
- They identify and overcome blocks to financial

freedom.

- They have an understanding and control of their own financial situation.
- They know how to sustain and expand whatever they have acquired.

Most importantly they are interested in freedom as much, if not more, than cash accumulation. They understand money and how it works. Most of all, they understand that money and wealth are not necessarily the same thing.

$$$

Before you can live the rich life you need to understand how people are motivated to use cash. Milton and Rose Friedman best explained this in their 1980 classic on economic liberty, "Free to Choose," in which The Nobel Prize winner in economics and his wife list the four ways that people spend cash. The following headings are from the Friedmans' book. The commentary is mine.

1. **You spend money on yourself.**
   You are motivated to get the thing you want most at the lowest price. This is the source of what I like to call "Bazaar Negotiating." You see something you want to buy. The dealer tells you what the price is but indicates that it is negotiable. The games begin. You make a counter cash or barter offer and you begin to nip and haggle until you believe you have gotten the best price you are going to get. The dealer, being no fool, will make a fair profit and allow you to make the purchase feeling as if you won.

2. **You spend your money on other people.**
   You still want the lowest price, you are less concerned in pleasing the recipient of your gift (unless you're in love or intensely concerned with "being fair"). You will still negotiate as hard as before but the choice of the item you are negotiating for can also be negotiated. You may want to get your friend that great car but if you cannot get the price you want for it you may decide to choose a different car. You are less likely to make this switch when the

purchase is for yourself.

3. **You spend other people's money on yourself.**
   You still want the goods and services more than ever but you are less or not at all concerned about obtaining the lowest price. You may even pay a higher price if someone else is picking up the cost so long as you get what you want.

4. **You spend other people's money on other people.**
   In this case, there is not much to negotiate for. You have neither a self interest in controlling the cost of the purchase nor in the actual goods and services being negotiated for. The only defining factor is your investment in pleasing those who have given you the money or who are receiving the goods and services being purchased.

Now that you have a better understanding of money, the next step will be to understand how money in its various forms creates wealth.

Understanding Wealth

Understanding wealth is not synonymous with understanding cash or money. In fact, most people are totally confused about the relationship between wealth, money, cash and thrift. Most would also be surprised to learn that actual wealth seldom has anything to do with how much cash a person has.

When questioned, Donald Trump, among the most studied examples of a "wealthy person," often states that he has no idea how wealthy he actually is. He is a builder with large real estate holdings and many related and unrelated holdings that are themselves constantly changing in value. Though he might be able to use many of these properties as collateral to increase his wealth, these for the most part are not liquid assets. In fact most of what Trump builds is built with OPM (Other People's Money). As wealthy as he appears to be after all the PR, hype and skilled marketing, Trump's wealth is really no more than a conglomeration of excess goods or and services.

Most individuals who fantasize of "being rich" have no distinction in their minds between stored wealth and the hyped, superficial wealth of an individual who can spend a few days at an expensive resort hotel and then go on a reckless, wasteful shopping spree on Rodeo Drive in Beverly Hills with nothing left to show for it when they are done. A review of the world's wealthiest people will show that they seldom define their own material wealth by how much cash they have. Instead their wealth generally consists of a combination of many things including some or all of the following;

- Precious stones

- Precious metals
- Artistic talent
- Jewelry (often created through the merging of precious stones, precious metals, and artistic talent)
- Valued works of art
- Influence
- Air rights
- Wisdom that creates influence
- Intellectual property including;
- Proprietary information, patents, and copyrights
- Social or business contacts
- Accumulation of land and the forests, woods and the trees and lumber upon it
- Metal, or oil in the land or ground
- Crops, livestock and water
- Silks, linens, wool, cotton
- Non-specific barterable resources
- Cash

Any of the above commodities and services can be traded for each other and often are. When necessary, for instance, for the payment of taxes, they can be converted to cash.

Which of the items listed above do you own or have access to?

Real wealth can create freedom. With wealth you can experience, do and have things with greater ease, in greater luxury, at the time of your own choosing, on your own terms.

Become an Alchemist of Money

Back in the middle ages some people believed you could turn lead to gold. That turned out to be false, but metaphorically, there is some truth to it. After all, one person's lead is another person's gold.

In other words, there is a way to live like a millionaire even if you don't have a million dollars. This involves replacing a million dollars in cash with a million dollars worth of comparable value.

Remember the old saying "time is money?" Have you ever heard of a person reducing expenses through sweat equity? Obtaining valuable items through intellectual currency? These are examples of time and physical energy being used as items of measurable value. The same can be said of space, information and emotional energy. These can also be used in place of cash as well. When you use these other factors instead of cash you are ssstttrrreeetttccchhhiiinnnggg your dollar.

If you use these factors skillfully you can take an income of $17,000 dollars and obtain a million dollars worth of goods and services with it. How? - Through the application of subtle influence.

Mathematicians know that there will be particular places where you can effect large changes with very little effort. This is known as leverage. Leverage comes about when there is profound understanding of the of all the interacting parts of a system by the concerned parties. Ultimately you have to put less energy into getting things at a lower cost. How is this done?

- By reducing cash outlay to about 5% of the value of what you eventually own, rent or borrow.

- By learning how to isolate obstacles to wealth eliminating or transcending them.
- If you can do these two things alone then if your income is $10,000 a year, you will be able to live like someone making $200,000 a year.
- I call this system of obtaining $20 dollars worth of goods and services for $1 dollar, “dollar stretching.”

The person who can effectively dollar stretch can live better on less than they ever imagined.

Delegate

Delegation is one of the most efficient means to increasing wealth while reducing your cash outflow. When you delegate, you are transferring a task, specific activity, a responsibility and a decision-making authority to another person. This transfer will be to a subordinate, to a friend, a family member and/or a business associate.

If delegation is done effectively it is empowering for all involved in the process.

- When you delegate you are free to use your time more effectively.
- Delegation funnels your personal strengths into tasks for which they are more suited.
- Delegation provides the one who delegates with a way to constrain their own behavior, i.e. limit their own weaknesses.
- Without delegation skills a person is likely to micromanage a project to their own detriment. An individual can place excessive energy into a project, reviewing, directing and reviewing again to the point of diminishing return.

To delegate well requires that you surround yourself with people who value excellence and respect the value of trust and integrity.

Support teams are essential to success in life, and the most effective support systems are those composed of people who keep their word. To delegate well, you must create relationships with people who do what they say they are going to do. When you delegate well, you reduce expenses by delegating chores to others who can do them for less money than your own time is worth.

When you delegate you may be conserving cash as well. Here is an exercise to get you started.

1. Identify how much money you earn for one hour of labor.
2. Divide your total weekly income by the hours you work weekly.
3. When you have determined know how much you make per hour, you can then delegate to others whose hourly rate is less or to someone who has a greater passion or skill for the task at hand.

Live Well Through Knowledge

The more effective you are at gathering information and trading it for what I like to call non-cash resources like influence, the less cash you need to spend in order to get the things you need. If you are ready to live rich then you will have to develop a simple but effective system for gathering, organizing, and using information. What is this system? Asking questions!

The inability or unwillingness to ask the right questions and act on the information is the major cause of poverty as well as a multitude of personal and social obstacles. Life, for the most part, is largely trial and error. The greater your level of knowledge, the greater your chances of success and a reduced chance of risk. Good knowledge helps you make better choices.

Here are some basic suggestions for mastering the art and science of wealth building knowledge? Spend an hour or two each day perusing through business and life-style magazines, The Wall Street Journal, Town and Country, Architectural Digest, GQ, the business and life-style section of the daily newspaper. Get Internet savvy. When you read a interesting article on style, search for more information using your favorite search engine on-line, and go into greater depth into the subject.

In time you will begin to develop a wide-ranging knowledge of the subject. With this knowledge and effective networking skills you can get access to those individuals who can open doors for you and introduce you to others of even greater influence. I call this process Vertical Networking. In Vertical Networking, you surround yourself with those more knowledgeable than yourself and spend time in conversation with them. When you listen to interviews with the best, brightest, and wealthiest in our society, you learn quickly that they are always gathering information that they can use to make wiser, more effective decisions. One of the easiest ways to gather valuable information is to learn from others and apply that information in your own life to increase your effectiveness. This Vertical Networking will bring you to mentors, people and places you would not have access to otherwise.

In the end, the ability to ask questions and develop powerful and strategic relationships will help you to work less, live better and enjoy more of what life has to offer.

$$$

II. THE MILLIONAIRE'S CODE

Building Your Live Rich System

To live rich you have to create a Live Rich System.

In a system, an established group of interdependent details - items, ideas, or principles - form a complex whole and maintain their existence by interacting regularly, harmoniously, orderly, and methodically over time to perform a task. For example one system in this book would focus on how to save cash on vacations. The subcategories here might include money conversions into foreign currencies, air fair, lodging, meals etc.

Making this system work effectively will require a balancing act between your mastery of the details of your life, your ways of doing things, your personal own unique style, and how these relate to creating the life you say you want to have.

The impact and influence that each part of the system laid out in this book exhibits will influence the whole Live Rich system. To apply this system feel free to begin with those tools and techniques that respond to your natural style but in the process of doing so, avoid overanalyzing the system. It is best to apply it as a whole.

$$$

Know Your Limitations

No matter how brilliant, wealthy, powerful, handsome, beautiful, or gifted you are, you will still have limitations. It is a great gift to have a healthy ego, and good self-esteem and still know your limitations.

The opposite of this is what is commonly called entitlement culture; the idea that you might deserve special treatment because of bad luck, bad genes, or unfortunate circumstances that have made your life more complicated than everyone else's. This is one of the primary reasons that people struggle unnecessarily. We all start out with limitations. Those who know how to live well possess sufficient insight and self-assessment skills to recognize their limitations. They have the ability to compensate for them as best they can, redirecting their strengths for maximum return on investment.

To learn your strengths and limitations you must begin a process of self-assessment. This is the process of gathering information about yourself, in order to make an informed decisions. After all, if you don't yet know where you are going, any road can take you there.

Begin the process by writing down the following:

- What are your greatest personality strengths?
- Can you leverage an excess of time, space, information or influence for something else?
- Are you comfortable emotionally in wielding power and influence?
- Are you skilled in taking risks and ending up ahead of the game?

The key question in dealing with your strengths and limitations is as follows:

If two choices have the same expected return, the one with the lower risk will be the best choice.

Knowing which choice has a lower risk is the defining factor between having wealth or unnecessary struggle. Without knowing your strengths and limitations you cannot make low-risk choices.

Money is nothing more than a store of value, and a medium of exchange. To act as a store of value, something must be able to be reliably saved, stored, and retrieved - and be predictably useful when it is so retrieved. Cash is only one of many commodities that function in this way.

Traditionally, when we speak of money, it is cash that comes to mind. This is a misnomer. Again, cash is only one type of money. Something that we trade for something else can be seen as a type of money as well. As such, there are many different forms of money, with their inherent strengths and weaknesses. This chapter will show the reader the different types of "non-cash" money.

- To live in a large building you do not need to be an architect or understand design.
- To drive a high performance car you do not need to be a skilled mechanic.
- To live like a millionaire on $17,000 does not require great cash wealth.

What living like a millionaire does require is your ability to live outside of the box of ordinary thinking about wealth, money and cash.

By learning how to leverage small amounts of cash with: time, your physical abilities, storage, living and working space, information and knowledge, influence and power, emotional energy, inner wisdom, clarity of thought, your consistency and dependability, and other people's barterable goods and services. With these things, you can create wealth and a quality of life that will transcend your wildest dreams.

Cash does not create wealth. Leveraging what you have and creating more from it, investing it, trading it, sharing it, influencing with it, will build your portfolio of value. It is like having a stock portfolio, or a real estate portfolio only what you have is a portfolio of $17,000 dollars, with all of the time, physical abilities, space, information, influence and power, emotional energy, inner wisdom, clarity of thought, consistency and dependability, and other people's barterable goods and services that you can accumulate or trade for.

These resources – non-cash currencies – combined with your clarity concerning your strengths and limitations will open the door to unlimited wealth.

Question? Which of the following types of money do you have the greatest access to?

- Cash?
- Promissory notes
- Smart cards
- Credit cards?
- Debit cards?
- Influence?
- Barterable goods and services?
- Time?
- Emotional Awareness/
  Consciousness
- Street smarts (common sense
- IOU
- Influence

How efficient are you at using these different types of money?

You Can Have it All, All of the Time If You Know What Having it All Means

I was having lunch with my friend Jonathan on a cold Sunday afternoon. Discussing this and that, I commented, "Well, you can't have it all, all of the time." Jonathan's response surprised me. "Of course you can have it all," he said, "But, you have to have an understanding of what having it all means."

He continued, "If you wanted a truly great Japanese meal, you could have it all. You'd find a five star Japanese restaurant, with great food, decor, service, etc. You'd bring people you really enjoy with you, and have this incredible Japanese meal. In that sense, you'd be having it all as far as Japanese food goes." Jonathan went on to point out that you can't make caviar out of a salami sandwich. So it is important to know the limits of what you are dealing with, whether it is your marital partner or a salami sandwich.

Generally speaking, unless you know (as Jonathan suggeseted) what "it all" is:

You can't have it all, all of the time.

You can, however, have some of it some of the time. You can even have all of it some of the time.

Consumer culture and its close relative short-term gratification run full time on the lie called You can have it all, all of the time.

Having it all is a lie - the worst kind of lie. It is the type of lie that people deny as it looks them directly in the eye. Most people know it's a lie but they live in denial, addicted to the feel-good of the moment and the fantasy that it will last forever.

My suggestion? Find out what you do have and learn to live with it and love yourself with it. That's as close as you are ever going to get to having it all. Live day to day with joy in every moment. Do it long enough and you'll be in a state of joy at the moment that you die. If you can do that then you will have had it all.

$$$

It is natural to avoid risk. Most people say no to incredible opportunities because they are afraid of the unknown risks. But if the benefit is worth it they may choose to act in spite of the risk.

If two choices have the same expected return, the one with lower risk will be the best choice. it. But how do we know which choice has a lower risk? This is hard to know if you are afraid of making any choice. In fact fear is probably the greatest obstacle to living well without cash - fear of risk, new ideas, fear of being different etc. Fear comes with a cost.

When reducing cash - and emotional - expenses it is important to reduce unnecessary risks. That means budgeting for Murphy's Law. What can go wrong will go wrong. Unexpected, unpleasant stuff happens and the results are costly. No matter what you do, where, when, or with whom, something may happen that will make you wish that you had done something else, someplace else, some other time, by yourself! If you can't avoid Murphy's Law, you can certainly budget for it. Always have a plan B, and a plan C, if you can't go with plan A. This will reduce the cost of everything.

There are two types of fear: healthy fear and unhealthy fear. A healthy fear might be driving a car with summer tires in a snowstorm. An unhealthy fear is that fear that cannot actually harm us or that we can do nothing about; dying of old age for instance. This type of fear is unhealthy, for it serves only to make us unhappy and paralyzes our need to make smart and effective choices.

Many people live in fear because they have a delusional or a distorted view of who they are seeing and of the world around them. Developing a sense of conservation and balance often reduces unhealthy fear.

$$$

Leveraging Your Emotional Responses For Building Wealth

Emotions are complex responses to an ever changing and unpredictable world. We must often survive by maintaining multiple motives while possessing limited capacities and resources for doing so effectively.

Robert Plutchik created one of the most influential classification approaches in the study of emotion with his eight primary emotions - anger, fear, sadness, joy, disgust, surprise, curiosity, and acceptance. This classification of emotions is important for our purposes because any one of them can motivate a person to invest resources, save, or spend money.

When it comes to choosing which of the ten non-cash currencies resources will serve us best in a particular place and time, it is important to keep in mind that even the most, reasonable, rational, sensible, probable and effective approaches to decision-making are based on our emotions. We may value one thing as opposed to another but this valuation is generally emotionally-driven. If you do not have a clear sense of what is truly of value to you and your emotional responses to different emotional stimuli, then you are destined to make a lot of poor financial decisions.

Effective decision-making involves merging what is rational, reasonable, practical and probable with the ability to compare the emotional worth of one thing over another. What we value is often based on the emotional worth we attribute to, and expect from the choices available to us.

Among the most effective ways to stop and reverse the escalation of negative emotional patterns is to recognize and acknowledge them. When an emotion is ignored, negated and repressed, it may transform into rage, a rage that can manifest through self-destructive habits.

The effective management of emotions can open the door to powerful strategic relationships, greater accessibility to the ten key resources and a sense of peace and contentment that can radically and positively influence buying and spending decisions.

Emotional energy as a non-cash currency to be bartered and traded is discussed further in Section Three.

III. APPLYING THE MILLIONAIRE'S CODE

Haste Makes Waste: The Art of Patience

It is one thing to have an understanding of a concept and another thing altogether to take that understanding and apply it in such a way as to radically upgrade your quality of life. Bringing understanding to action requires information, motivation and emotional clarity.

A person who can manage their emotions is less inclined to make poor short-term choices and comfort-based decisions. They know that patience often leads to the bigger prize. With patience you can effectively balance the non-cash currencies; time, space, cash, physical energy, and emotional energy. The greater your self-awareness concerning each resource, the greater your patience and the less struggle you will experience.

$$$

It isn't always clear when to wait and when to act. Sometimes haste makes waste, and sometimes a stitch in time saves nine. Emotional clarity, intuition and the ability to think before acting will guide you towards the correct actions.

We must beware of the obsession with I want this now. The solution? Patience.

Patience is the ability to endure waiting, delay, or provocation without becoming annoyed or upset. With patience you can persevere calmly when faced with difficulties. Why is patience so important to living the rich life? Because the cash cost for urgency is always higher than waiting.

The cure for impatience is to put off impulse purchases. Also, whenever possible make substitutions of one thing for another (for example, burn CDs you get from the public library onto your computer and transfer your mixes to blank CDs).

Most people, driven by misplaced and misdirected pride, vanity, ambition, and a hunger to own more and more, will push things so that when the point of excess is reached, they are burdened by the resulting crises. Learn, instead, to conserve and balance; and abundance will be the result.

$$$

Wu Wei and the Law of Attraction

In traditional Chinese philosophy there is a concept known as Wu Wei: "the action that does not-interfere." This is a world-view that is difficult to understand for a person who believes that struggle is a necessary element of day-to-day living.

But this non-action, Wu Wei, can be an active rather than passive process. It is not about achievement through laziness or resignation to circumstance. Rather, it requires a focused and attentive mind and clear consciousness that enables one to eliminate unnecessary action. Through this attentive mind comes an ability to manifest what is needed at any particular moment. It is the ultimate expression of getting what you need, just when you need it and having it be what you want.

Wu Wei is the law of attraction, the concept of build-it-and-they-will-come in the blockbuster movies The Secret, and Field of Dreams. This is what we see when a bird flies on the thermals, wings spread out, rising higher and higher but never flapping its wings. In Wu Wei, the things that we are most ready, willing and able to do, we do without thought.

If you are committed to living a rich life, it is important to take a few moments every morning and explore those things that are important to you and express your passions, and then do those things. This exercise will bring you want you want and need, and is only as difficult as taking a deep breath.

Remember, Wu Wei does not imply that there is value in doing nothing. To live in the world is to act. Wu Wei means to act without attachment, without emotional investment. It implies going with the flow of natural law without trying to control or take charge of that flow. This action through non-action is actually the path to emotional and material freedom.

Once you have a sense of your strengths and limitations, and once you define just how much cash you have to spend, and which of the ten non-cash currencies are most accessible, the next step is to master the art of conserving and balancing. When is it time to save for later, and can you spend now?

A good way to begin this process is to become familiar with Pareto's Principle. Vilfredo Pareto, an Italian economist at the turn of the 20th century, observed that that twenty percent of the Italian people at that time owned eighty percent of their country's accumulated wealth.

Over time Pareto's Principle, also known as the 80/20 rule, was used to specify virtually any relationship where the energy extended appeared unequal to the results achieved. In the century or so since Pareto conducted his research, his principle has come to explain that, for many phenomena, 20% of invested input or causative factor is responsible for 80% of the results or consequences. This principle is a key factor in the creation of cash-free wealth. Even the wealthy person must be able to conserve and balance their wealth.

The Pareto Principle of 80/20 can be applied in a wide range of areas: athletics, teamwork, scientific research and the Alchemy of Wealth as described throughout this book.

$$$

Learn to Play the Zero Sum Game

Sometimes in life there is one of something, and many people with plenty of resources who all want that one thing. This is called a Zero Sum Game.

Imagine that you are at a party and they are serving the greatest apple pie in the world, baked by an award winning dessert chef. The pie is divided into eight slices. There are twelve people of varying incomes who want a slice of the pie. Eight slices of pie – twelve people.

You love apple pie! If cash is the only acceptable payment, those willing to pay the most for the piece of pie will probably get a slice. Those four who are less willing to pay the most for the slices will go home pie-less. Now imagine that the four individuals left out of the pie game have great entrepreneurial skills and are thinking of ways to get a slice of the pie without spending cash. With creativity, initiative, and research one of those four could find something of greater value to the dessert chef than cash alone. By isolating some other variables such as time, space, delegation skills, influence, networking skills, initiative, information or barter it is entirely possible, even likely, that he could get a piece of the pie. In fact, if what he had to offer the chef was valuable enough he might even persuade the chef to pay him to take a slice of the pie. He might get the chef to bake a whole new pie and pay him to take it!

The Zero Sum Game factor is an element of commerce that is common in all business but more so in cash-based transactions. Patience grants you clarity, and clarity can help you to maneuver when your options seem limited. You can transcend the zero sum game by reducing risk and maximizing non-cash resources. Each time you are able to increase the value to another person of what you have and exchange that thing or combination of things for something you want you automatically free up cash. You can then use that cash where it will have the greatest value to you.

So where does risk reduction fit in? An understanding of risk affects virtually every aspect of our lives. A balanced risk evaluation system will enable you to clarify what choices are or not safe, reduce your personal struggle, and maximize benefits.

When assessing risk you have to first define your assets- essentially what would be at risk if you made a poor choice? Where are your vulnerabilities, what would the loss be; what would the estimated cost of recovery be? Then you must summarize of possible defensive measures to reduce risk and the costs and estimated savings from better risk management. This will give you the upper hand in any zero sum situation.

$$$

Save Cash by Trading What You Have for What You Want

When you trade one thing for another it is called barter. In this type of trading, goods or services are given a specific value and are exchanged for a certain number or amount of other goods and services of equal value. Little or no cash is involved in the transaction.

The amazing thing about this approach to business is that it utilizes all of the traditional methods for creating wealth and economic freedom talked about in all those how to get rich books and tapes, but does it without cash.

Surprisingly, people of great wealth conduct much more business through barter than they do with cash. The greater a person's wealth, the greater the probability that he or she uses many different forms of non-cash currency to create and recreate wealth.

As I said earlier in the book, cash is only one type of money. There are many different forms of money; each with their inherent strengths and weaknesses. For the past two thousand years, cash has been the most popular form of money, but it was never the only form of money. In the 21st century, cash is becoming increasingly less popular. Clearly, there are more different types of money available than ever before. As confusing as this fact may be to someone who thinks of money only in terms of cash, it is a fact.

Now is the time for you to think outside of the box.

Create a new paradigm and see money as it actually functions in the world. When we speak of barter we are thinking big. Please do not imagine a farmer trading chickens for loaves of bread. Think about buying plane tickets and living in a Five Star Resort Spa. Trading the ten non-cash currencies – physical abilities, space, information, influence and power, emotional energy, inner wisdom, clarity of thought, consistency and dependability, and other people's barterable goods and services can help you:

- Conserve cash by profiting at full retail price from the sale of distressed, obsolete, outdated, excess or slow-moving inventory.
- Benefit in contract negotiations.
- Reduce your taxable cash income.
- Get interest free loans without borrowing money from a bank.
- Dramatically increase your chances of success when presented with a zero sum game.

Right now, the world economy is in radical transformation due to the billions of dollars in barter credits changing hands. Will you make the leap to living well or be left behind to struggle?

Note: Direct barter can have a frontier-like, anarchist element to it since anything goes and laws and rules are few and far between. Reputations, good and bad, travel fast and it is wise to avoid troublemakers and those who cannot be trusted. When both parties cannot make and trade immediately try whenever possible to get your needs met first and deliver your good and service later. This will protect you from being taken advantage of.

$$$

Save Cash by Trading: Master the 10 Non-Cash Currencies

We have spoken throughout this book about the ten non-cash currencies. Hard as it might be to believe, most of the business transactions you have completed in your life have been done with very little or no cash. You may not have thought about this, but millionaires think about it all the time. What the wealthy use, and what you have often used yourself, is a combination of cash and ten non-cash resources. This section will help you to master these wealth-building tools. Spend a few days on each one, and begin applying them in your life instead of cash.

1. Time
2. Physical energy
3. Space
4. Information
5. Influence
6. Emotional energy
7. Spiritual Focus
8. Clarity of thought
9. Dependability
10. Reciprocal Trade (Barter of goods and services)

When it comes to choosing which of the ten key resources will serve us best in a particular place and time, it is important to keep in mind the following:

The fastest way to reduce the amount of cash needed to live well and become wealthy is to assess the Ten Cashless Currencies and find those that most connect to your vision, personal passion and individual style.

If you do not have a clear sense of what and what isn't truly of value to you, you are destined to make a lot of bad financial decisions. As I said in an earlier chapter, all decision-making is based on valuation. How we value something is, more often than not, based on the emotional worth we attribute to, and expect from the choices available to us.

In previous sections of this book I gave you the basic principles for using your mind to grow rich. The following sections are designed to show you how to apply attention to detail, your well-honed intuitive capabilities, the right information, and strategic relationships in making amazingly accurate, wealth-producing decisions based on the shifting value of the Ten Cashless Currencies.

Even the most, reasonable, rational, sensible, probable and effective approaches to decision-making are based on how we value one thing as opposed to another.

If you are looking to create wealth and do more than just save some cash by being frugal and thrifty, then studying and mastering the next section of the book is essential. It will maximize all of your talents and help to magnify your passions.

Enjoy the ride!

$$$

IV. THE ALCHEMY OF WEALTH

Clarity of Thought

One cannot discuss the mystery of wealth without first discussing the mind. The mind, still perhaps the greatest of all mysteries, is at the center of our very existence, yet not even the greatest scientists are really sure what it is or how it functions.

Creating wealth through clarity of thought integrates a wide range of functions and activities including intellect, consciousness, perception, memory, emotion, will, and imagination.

Knowledge is power, but effective learning is not just gathering information. If you to be successful and achieve your goals and dreams, then you will have to both study and organize information and learn to create wealth through the actions you take based on that information. Life is largely trial and error. The greater your level of knowledge, the greater your chances of success with a reduced chance of risk.

No matter how well developed one's knowledge is and how many hours have been dedicated to a particular area of study, the ability to apply that knowledge is the defining factor. If the knowledge cannot be applied, then it cannot create results. And what is the essential factor in applying knowledge? It is clarity of thought.

$$$

Time

Time is money, and yet for many people, it is nothing more than that. Time is a concept, a belief, and an ever-shifting experience. The ability to manage, shape and use time effectively is a key to creating wealth. When you are able to control your time well, you immediately increase your effectiveness, able to accomplish essential tasks at the lowest cost.

The timeliness of friends and business associates can affect your cost of doing business. Time can be given a cash value. This is defined by how, where, and with whom you spend your time. In fact time may be one of the most underrated of the cashless currencies.

If you value your time, and want to live rich, you must define the cash value of each thing you do, whether it is washing dishes, or waiting around at the airport for a delayed flight. You must develop skills for handling urgent projects, and integrate non-urgent responsibilities, and trivial needs into your daily schedule before they become urgent.

The master of time knows that some details that seem trivial in the short run can prove quite essential over time.

Remember, the more time you have, the more freedom you have to reduce the amount of cash that will be required to get what you need. For example:

- Whenever you plan on going somewhere, estimate the time it will take you to get there and add 30% more time for the task. For example, if you are going to an appointment, and the travel time is about an hour, budget an hour and twenty minutes for the journey...

Use time to prepare yourself for unlimited possibilities:

- Choose a time of day that you believe will be most creative for you. Working alone, re-write your vision on paper, listing as many specific details as possible. Create various scenarios.

$$$

Physical Energy

Sometimes what you have available as currency to get what you want is physical energy; whether your own or the energy or information of someone whose energy you can borrow through delegation. The use of physical energy as a form of payment is known as sweat equity. Sweat equity describes the contribution or compensation made to a project with time and effort in replacement of cash. A specific dollar amount can be applied to evaluate the value of the sweat equity provided, or the sweat equity may allow a purchaser to do work in place of all or part of the down payment and other costs of a purchase.

Sweat equity can help you become a partner in a business when you are not contributing financial capital. In many start up businesses, employees might, upon incorporation, be paid stock, stock options, or ownership shares in exchange for working for a below-market salary.

The term sweat equity is also often used to describe the increased value of real estate when owners make improvements by their own labor. The more labor and the specific type of labor applied to the home, and the greater the resultant increase in value, the greater value of the sweat equity that has been applied. By using sweat equity of greater value you can reduce your cash investment in virtually any project. So, how can you apply sweat equity? Know what your time is worth, per week, per month, per hour etc.

The application of sweat equity is also relevant to creating a millionaire life-style. Don't labor at tasks that you can barter or pay others to do at a rate that is less than your pay rate.

Don't lick your own stamps if your time is worth $20

an hour! Hire a kid for minimum wage to lick your stamps. This will free you up to create more cash income for yourself or give you more time to play.

$$$

Space

Many of the things that are of greatest value to us and in the marketplace need to be stored until their value increases.

Just think about it. We use our memory to store the record of our experiences; we store knowledge in books and books in libraries. We store things in locker rooms, coat-rooms, attics, basements and the type of luggage storage areas found in train stations, amusement parks, and airports. All these things have values that increase and decrease over time.

The population is growing, society is more consumer-driven than ever, apartments are smaller, and space to store things has become scarcer and scarcer.

Your ability to store your own property, energy and ideas as well as the property, energy, and ideas of others can be a great tool for creating wealth. The greater your skill at organizing your personal clutter and isolating and evaluating your access to storage of all forms will help you to effectively invest your cash-less currency resulting in greater wealth.

1. Take four boxes and label them A, B, and C.
2. Gather all of your papers together, especially from the piles that one might call clutter.
3. The papers that need to be addressed in the next twenty-four hours should be placed in box A.
4. Papers that do not require action for at least a week should be placed in box B.
5. Papers that don't require action for at least a month should be placed in box C.
6. Papers that do not require action for at least six

months should be stored. Take them out in five months and return them to the system.

7. This is a highly effective system especially if you are a pack rat who is unlikely to change your ways anytime soon.

$$$

Information

If you look at your own life you'll see that even the grandest project depends on the success of the smallest components. If you look at the world around you, you will see that even the largest mountain is made up of sand, pebbles, compressed dirt; in other words, small stuff. A grand project cannot succeed if the smallest components are dysfunctional or out of balance. The smallest detail, if missing or out of place, can cause large-scale failure, regardless if it's a military campaign or balancing a checkbook. Getting organized can help you reduce the cost of repeating projects and buying products that you already have, but have misplaced.

Here are a few thoughts on the power of information to create wealth:

If you are not internet savvy learn to use this valuable tool for gathering information. When you read a interesting article, search using your favorite online search engine and go into greater depth into the subject. In time you will begin to develop a wide ranging knowledge of the world that will enable to you vertically network with greater effectiveness. This will bring you to people and places you would not have access to otherwise.

My suggestions for gaining this powerful knowledge from the media: Listen to National Public Radio, watch Charlie Rose on National Educational Television (NET), Ovation – a cable channel dedicated to the arts, Democracy Now with Amy Goodman, 60 Minutes and CBS Sunday Morning, also important television shows.

- Research information that will help you go to the next step.

- In social situations keep your opinion to yourself unless asked and avoid speaking from a different point of view. Remember you are gathering information, not having a debate. Avoid provoking a defensive response.
- With another person's permission ask probing questions to draw out their reasoning. Find out as much as you can about why they are saying what they are saying.
- Check to be sure that you are really understanding what they are saying.
- Don't ask another question for a few seconds. Allow what they have said to sink in.
- If someone disagrees with you, instead of saying "What's your proof?" ask, "I need your help in understanding your thinking here." Ask "Why is this important? Can you give me an example?"
- Repeat what they have said as you understand. You can ask, "Am I correct that you're saying such and such?"

The truth about accumulating information and knowledge:

- We are all students.
- All students can learn.
- All students need and deserve the highest quality education.
- All students must be challenged to perform to the best of their abilities.
- All genuine knowledge is active, not passive.

- Those who have knowledge have a fundamental need to share that knowledge.
- All knowledge is accessible if the student is ready, willing and able.

As you learn more about the remaining non-cash currencies, remember that information and influence are the two factors other than cash that can give you specificity and urgency

Influence

Influence is the ability to indirectly control or affect the actions of other people or things. The greater your influence, the less cash you must to spend to get what you need, and the more cash you can save for the future.

Plain and simple, the accumulation and application of influence can get you to places and create wealth that cash alone never could, can't now, and never will.

The key to creating wealth with a minimum of cash is to gain greater control of your external environment. When you are skilled at controlling your external environment, you can gain instant access to what you want or need. Cash can be often replaced with influence.

When individuals focus on common interests, their attention and the interaction between them will naturally flow to present and future interests, and away from obstacles and past regrets.

In all human interactions, there are complex multiple, shared, isolating, compatible, conflicting points of interest and agreement as well as areas of general rapport that are essential elements for creating an environment where influence is effectively utilized.

It's not what you know; it's whom you know. And what you know about whom you know can become a fountain of wealth, power and influence.

In our daily lives, influence can be a highly effective instrument of power and prestige. Power and prestige can be achieved through the access to and integration and application of various qualities, the most prominent being the intention, mental clarity, authority, physical strength and speed required to do something or get something done.

In their most extreme forms, power and prestige imply the ability to impose one's will on others, even if those others resist in some way. However, when influence is employed correctly, it efficiently moves people in positive directions. If you wish to create and sustain positive change in others while accumulating great wealth, then you will need to study how the influence process works.

$$$

Emotional Energy

Most of the choices we make, especially poor choices, are driven more by how we feel than by what we think. In fact, neurological research suggests that the emotions are an essential aspect of how humans plan, make decisions and behave.

Emotional responses are never neutral. They are positive or negative, appropriate or inappropriate. In the end, how we respond emotionally to situations and people has an important effect on our quality of life; to live rich.

It is important that we somehow nudge or influence our emotional choices in directions that serve us best. It is emotions, when guided through finely tuned intuition and available evidence, that will help us to make the best choices.

Psychiatrist William Glasser theorizes that behavior is composed of four simultaneous factors: deeds, ideas, emotions, and physiological states. What we do as human beings is choose an idea and then act upon it. While this is happening, associated emotions and physiological states also occur but these cannot be chosen independently. This is why we may wish to control our behavior and yet we often can't.

Simply put, most shopping decisions - impulse purchases in particular - and decisions wherein we choose to either live our lives in great wealth or poverty, are emotional in nature.

I use the following affirmations to keep me emotionally grounded:

1. I deserve love and respect.

2. My ability to receive love is determined by what I believe I deserve to receive.
3. Everything in life involves change and transformation. Whether or not I choose transformation, everything is transformed by time.
4. My desire for habit and comfort is an essential part of the human condition. I will not judge myself for these desires.
5. Without a vision or a mission, life seems aimless.
6. Life is not a series of lessons to be learned. It is a series of messages to be heard. If I hear the message, I won't have to learn the lesson.
7. Willpower and discipline without vision or a sense of purpose is struggle.
8. Success happens at the very moment that preparation and an opportunity meet.

What are emotions? The word "emotion" is commonly used yet there is no one, commonly accepted definition for what an emotion is. If nothing else, emotional responses, whether sadness, joy, love or fear, motivate us to act and continue acting. The origin of this motivation is generally hidden from conscious inspection. Even so, emotionally driven action is necessary for even the most rational actions.

Emotions color most of the choices we make, so the more you understand your emotions, the wiser you become concerning what you choose to buy and when you choose to buy it. Some of our poorest choices are made in response to our emotional memories. What is the purpose of having great wealth if you don't even know who you are?

It is essential that you transcend irrational emotional resistance and spiritual scarcity if you want to live rich on very little cash.

$$$

Inner Wisdom

Wealth cannot be created and sustained unless you possess inner wisdom; a combination of emotional intelligence and spiritual clarity. You must harness your natural emotional responses in order to create cash free wealth and both emotional and spiritual contentment.

It is important to remember that as you create wealth and abundance in your life, you must first do so with your head and heart in the right place. Spirituality means different things to different people. After all, there are atheists who act more spiritually than those who claim to be spiritually motivated. And what exactly is a spiritual person anyway? There are thousands of religions theories, beliefs, rites and rituals - all working towards the same goal – Self or God realization. A common denominator that might link everyone's idea of spirituality would be a devotion to activities that motivate, inspire, renew, uplift, comfort, and serve a spiritual ideal.

A financially secure, purpose driven, spiritually focused life is a life filled with inspiration, insight and inner wisdom. It is a life filled with contentment and rich in physical pleasure, creativity and culture, in all its forms.

Dependability

Much of what is involved in living rich is based on dependability - dependability that something will have a certain value, will function as promised, or will produce a certain result. Dependability is the end result of a relationship of reliance, one based on trust.

We often make the mistake of believing that a trusted party should have good character, vices, or morals. This is mistake since even persons engaged in a criminal activity usually trust each other to some extent. Also, trust does not need to include an action that you and the other party are mutually engaged in. Trust is a prediction of reliance on an action, based on what a party knows about the other party. Trust is a statement about what is otherwise unknown - for example we trust that something will happen even if it is far away, cannot be verified, or is in the future.

We can try to statistically isolate how trustworthy a party we are depending on may or may not be, but ultimately when dealing with human beings or organizations (like the government), trust is a mental state that cannot be measured directly. Confidence in the results of trusting may be measured through behavior, or alternatively, one can measure self-reported trust. An example of self reported trust might be major league baseball promising to control steroid use among its players; then creating a report. Trust may be considered a moral choice or at least an intuitive one, allowing the human to deal with complexities that rationalistic reasoning cannot address.

There is one scenario where trust and dependability can be measured to some degree of accuracy provided moral behavior does not come into the equation - this is in machine-human trust. Machines and computers have no moral sense and rely on rational computations, yet you can reasonably determine how successful they will be at doing your taxes, or landing on the moon. However, even here you must determine, how dependable the creator of the machine or device is for they are the ones who have implemented the rational rules into the device.

If you are skilled at transferring resources - physical, financial, intellectual, or temporal - to another, and have the influence and the skill to make them behave in dependable ways then you have tremendous power to control the many variables than can help you to live rich.

$$$

Barterable Goods and Services

We've explored the fundamentals of trading and barter in Section Two. Barter has been a wonderful tool for doing business for thousands of years, but there were always limitations. These included:

- Barterable goods had to be stored.
- The value of barterable goods was subject to change due to uncontrollable circumstances.
- Barterable goods could be damaged, stolen or destroyed by fire, flooding or attacks by insects or animals.
- Bulky commodities could not be protected or hidden from robbers or tax collectors as easily as cash.
- Minted coinage eliminated the difficulty of accurately measuring commodities.
- In earlier times there was no standardization in the size of the jars in which oil and grain were stored. Only estimates were possible. Standardized weights and scales, even when available, were few and difficult to obtain.
- Unlike cash, dealing with barterable goods may have required the use of a middleman due to extraordinary needs.
- A needed product or service may not have been available at the time.

But things have changed dramatically in the last three decades. In the past centuries the ability to use barter as a primary tool of wealth was limited by the inability of third parties to connect. Now the use of barter brokers and the introduction of barter tracking software have made it much easier to do large barter deals between individuals or organizations that have never met.

Throughout the following sections you will find many ways to use barter along with the other ten non-cash currencies for creating wealth.

$$$

OBSTACLE$

V. THE OBSTACLES AND BOTTLENECKS

Understanding Obstacles

In order to live well with very little cash you must clearly, continually, and directly focus on maximizing your potential to produce wealth and avoid or eliminate the obstacles that may arise.

An obstacle, for our purposes, is any random thing that interferes with your ability to utilize and maximize all of the ten non-cash currencies needed to live well with little or no cash. Obstacles may be emotional, circumstantial, psychological, physical, historical, cultural, gender-based, etc.

Developing an effective low-cash approach to living very well would be simple except for random obstacles. Random shifts and changes in interdependent resources must be addressed. After all, the value of each non-cash currency may suddenly increase or decrease for any number of reasons. Examples of such random shifts might include but are not limited to: changing of frequent flyer rules, addition of hidden fees by credit cards companies, hurricanes in Florida, scarcity of something you want, changes in the marketplace, your local thrift store has raised all their prices on everything...

The fact is that all the different resources in the system of living well without cash are connected. There are specific self-created obstacles that can short circuit the wealth-building process. The most common ones are:

- Poor time management skills
- Poor or negative attitude
- Poor self assessment system

- Multiple priorities with multiple deadlines
- Perfectionism
- Lack of long-term vision

Bottlenecks

When an unexpected, sudden devaluation of one of the ten non-cash currencies takes place, it influences the value of the other nine currencies. This can slow down the entire wealth building process by creating a jam-up, or what I call a bottleneck. Just as a car slowing down to change lanes, for instance, may cause a traffic jam, so any event or circumstance, no matter how seemingly insignificant, can cause a bottleneck.

Here is an exercise to help you understand just what a bottleneck is:

1. Take any empty bottle that has a small opening. It can be a soda bottle or a juice bottle.
2. Now fill this bottle with water.
3. Standing over a sink turn the bottle upside down.
4. Now watch how the liquid pours out. You can see air bubbles inside the bottle as the liquid pours out unevenly.
5. You can see that there is more water in the jar than the small opening will allow to pour out at once.

In a sense you could say that there is an abundance of water, more than can be processed through the opening.

Now, there are always going to be obstacles and the resulting bottlenecks. That's how life works. We may not always know what they are, but they will be there nonetheless. In order to get to next step you must identify the bottleneck and the obstacle that has created it. Then you must transcend or eliminate it before the process of living rich can go forward.

In the rare situation where you cannot eliminate an obstacle you will have to learn to transcend it. Warren Gresches, a noted speaker on the issue of obstacles says "You go over, under, around or through them!"

$$$

The Art and Science of Assessments

One of the essential requirements to maximizing the effort you put into living rich is the ability to measure what is commonly called ROI or return on investment. This is the amount of benefit you receive, greater then the amount of resources you expend. Corporations spend millions of dollars a year on consultant services designed to isolate this specific information.

Through self-assessment you can regularly critique your buying, selling and saving patterns. You can review clearly your greatest assets and isolate areas in which improvements can be made. Then as you actively engage the process of increasing your income and reducing your expenses you can monitor the ten key resources, recognize which ones are at their highest values and which are at their lowest values and isolate or utilize each accordingly.

Self-assessment should not be a struggle. Focus on those skills that come to you with the greatest ease and which can be mastered most readily.

To start practicing the simple assessment skill you can start with prioritizing your day.

At the beginning of each day:

- Identify what you really want to accomplish.
- Set short- and long-range goals.
- Arrange the items according to their importance.
- Create a to-do list with the higher priority items listed first.
- Take care of higher priority items first thing in the morning.

- Save low priority items for later in the day.

Applying self-assessment techniques is a process of learning to respect the details. It is key that you keep accurate records. Save receipts and keep track of your daily cash buys. File these receipts in a manila envelope or folder until you need them.

Remember, making financially-based and quality of life choices without some assessment exercise is similar to buying a stock or real estate on a guess. Assess and assess again. Then act!

$$$

How We Create Our Own Financial Bottlenecks

An old cartoon called Pogo once had a character saying, "We have discovered the enemy and it is us!" How true that is!

Following is a simple assessment exercise to help isolate obstacles that can lead to bottlenecks.

Ask yourself which of these descriptions applies to you. Write down how frequently one of these sentences describes you, ranging from "not at all" to "always."

- Procrastination
- Disorganization
- Misplaced items
- Interruptions
- Lack of information
- Incorrect information
- Too many commitments
- Unnecessary correspondence
- Inability to say "No"
- Dysfunctional need to please others
- Poor listening skills
- Confusing socializing with networking
- Excessive socializing
- Unwillingness to be accountable for errors you've committed
- Other people's mistakes
- Excess Micromanaging
- Poor delegation skills
- Weak support systems
- Understaffing on projects
- Lack of feedback
- Changing of external factors
- Changing of internal priorities

- No goals or misdirected goals and objectives

$$$

The Three Primary Types of Obstacles

Obstacles come in many types, shapes and forms. Some are a reflection of our own internal limitations while others are external; a reflection of events, circumstances and the environment that surrounds us. Whichever they are, they can lead to bottlenecks that keep us from reaching our goals. What they all have in common is that they reduce effectiveness, freedom and increase the amount of cash required to to live well.

As there are systems in all aspects of life, there is also a system for organizing and classifying obstacles. Generally speaking there are three primary types of obstacles.

1. Internal resource obstacles, or as I like to call them, IROs. Poor time management skills, shyness, or emotional resistance from a childhood trauma are all IROs.
2. When there is an internal resource obstacle, it will control the accessibility to and the effectiveness of the other nine non-cash currencies.
3. Obstacles that are created by changes in the external environment or marketplace: I call these market driven obstacles (MDOs). Market driven obstacle exists when the demand for a good or service increases or decreases in such a way as to negatively influence your ability to obtain it at the lowest possible cash cost. It is very difficult, for example to buy a reduced priced gift on Christmas Eve, or buy an inexpensive hot dog at a ball game or at an airport restaurant. You are stuck buying the hot dog at the price they are asking. The controlled

scarcity of the hot dog increases the price but this MDO is out of your ability to influence.

4. Belief based obstacles (BBOs). These are the rules, procedures and paradigms we create from myths, religious faith or cultural patterns that we consciously choose to accept. BBOs often interfere with our productivity and effectiveness especially in utilizing the ten cashless-currencies. In order to reduce the influence of BBOs a person must apply self-assessment tools. This will help the individual to identify patterns that will create of obstacles. The most common patterns are ordinary thinking, fear of failure, surrounding yourself with negative, unsupportive people, and believing that paying attention to certain details just isn't that important.

$$$

Isolating Bottlenecks

Individuals who are disorganized or who are reactive to external circumstances will often complain that that there are too many obstacles for them to handle. They are in a state of overwhelm. They may genuinely feel victimized by circumstances, but more often than not, it is they, the individual responsible for decision-making who creates the obstacle. It may be that they focus on the wrong resources at the wrong time, delegate ineffectively, lack essential skills, make the wrong choices, or it is simply a belief-based obstacle. In time however, when applying this unique process they learn that it was only one obstacle leading to a bottleneck that created the illusion of many obstacles. As soon as the primary obstacle was removed or the bottleneck expanded the effectiveness of all the resources in the system expanded radically.

In order to create an active, functional cash-free wealth building system, it is essential that you isolate those obstacles that can create or contribute to the formation of bottlenecks. You must isolate their under-lying causes - issues like quality, price, availability, and then determine the reasons why they might lead to a bottleneck.

The non-cash currency of time is of greatest value here because it is important to reduce the amount of time wasted in isolating or expanding a bottleneck. The way to avoid wasting valuable time is to understand as much as possible the relationship between an action and the effect of that action- cause-effect.

Here is a brief summary of how you can reduce obstacles and create a huge reserve of cashless wealth through teamwork.

- You will need to form a group of friends and colleagues, individuals with different strengths and talents who understand the concept of the Ten Cashless Currencies.

- The group must choose a facilitator who will guide the group in the creation of an implementation plan.

The Five Secret Steps to Eliminating Obstacles

There is a saying that the truth you ignore will come back to bite you on the butt! As you address obstacles, be prepared to subordinate everything else in the process to it.

Discovering obstacles that are slowing down the process of cash-free wealth building is an important skill. This skill can be developed through the use of what are called assessment tools. The most popular assessment tool is the questionnaire. Assessment Questionnaires, many of which are placed throughout this book can help you recognize your strengths and weaknesses as well as previously unknown and unrecognized obstacles. Once an obstacle has been isolated it can be eliminated or compensated for. This results in the shifting of the bottleneck. Without the obstacle and the bottleneck to slow the process, the wealth will flow.

In the chapter on removing bottlenecks, we learned that the facilitator needs to understand cause and effect and have the ability to recognize and isolate an obstacles when it appears. There are five key steps for eliminating obstacles. These are to:

1. Identify the obstacles and bottlenecks by evaluating all ten of the key resources (non-cash currencies).
2. Identify the obstacle to actually increase efficiency.
3. Minimize all other resources that are connected to the obstacle and the bottleneck.
4. Expand the useful properties of the obstacle as a way of eliminating the bottleneck or at the very least increasing the capacity of the

bottleneck.

5. Regularly repeat the process since a new obstacle may arise to create a new bottleneck that may require further action.

When an obstacle is removed from the wealth building process you immediately save more cash then you could save by just randomly looking for discounted items, visiting sales in retail outlets or just thinking frugally. Why? Because through assessing, isolating and removing obstacles you are isolating the root factor of the bottleneck. You are ending the wasteful and ineffective use of cash. In doing so you are shifting your attention and physical and emotional energy to converting non-cash mediums such as influence or information to get what you want.

$$$

Too Much Abundance Can Create Obstacles to Cashless Wealth

Can a person have too much wealth? The answer is yes! Hard as it is to believe, sometimes the greatest obstacle of all is having more than we need or want. In such a situation the obstacle is excess abundance.

Let me explain. The problem is actually that people - we might call them Type A personalities - focus on gathering more and more of the Ten Cashless Currencies. They do this without a break, without rest or relaxation, all the purpose of maximizing the performance of every one of these resources all the time. This is actually an impossible task. It requires time and emotional energy that are way beyond the point of any benefit that might result from this activity. Essentially they are putting out more than they are getting. This rather than creating greater productivity, results in a wasteful and draining effect on the entire cashless wealth building process.

What is required here, and is usually lacking is: proper assessment skills, an understanding of the three types of obstacles and the ability to apply the five key steps for eliminating obstacles. A metaphor for this situation would be a bird constantly, unnecessarily flapping it's wings an attempt to go ever higher, even though there is plenty of wind and it could easily ride the thermals – spirals of warm air rising up to great heights.

There are many wealthy people who work excessively long hours. They don't have time for their families, have no hobbies and are very narrowly focused. The have lots of adult toys but are generally dissatisfied. They put out lots of energy, and are wealthy by all traditional definitions, and yet they definitely put out more than they get back.

They are wing flappers, unnecessarily flapping their wings.

They need to learn how to fly on the wind and rise on the thermals.

Are you a wing flapper or a thermal rider?

$$$

VI. *FROM OBSTACLES TO ASSETS*

More on Conservation and Balance

As is described in depth in an earlier chapter on Conservation and Balance, an ideal lifestyle is a balanced lifestyle. Once you have assessed your strengths and limitation, once you understand bottlenecks, and obstacles, can define just how much cash your have to spend, and which of the ten non-cash currencies are most accessible, then you are on your way. But there is a natural, intuitive next step.

At this point you must be able to adjust your lifestyle choices to the existence of imbalance in the relationship of each of the Ten Cash Currencies to one another. For instance you may have more information than you need at a particular time and place, but little influence; plenty of space but no demand for it; plenty of time but nothing to do with that time...

Conservation and balancing skills may assist you in bypassing certain obstacles and using problem solving and obstacle-removing skills to increase your productivity and reduce uncontrollable variables that can increase your cash expenditures. It is as if you hear about a traffic jam on the highway and simply go off onto the exit ramp for a smooth ride, only going back on the highway when the bottleneck has been bypassed.

Generally, we look for the biggest, most obvious problem or obstacle in our path. After all it is more comfortable to look for the obvious problem rather than looking for a needle in a haystack. But when dealing with obstacles and bottlenecks, everything might not be as it seems. The obvious may not meet the eye. Often addressing obstacles and bottlenecks becomes a counter-intuitive process.

Each of the Ten Cashless Currencies have obstacles associated with them. It would be easier if there were one big obstacle that could just be removed. This is not, however how obstacles arise. They are seldom permanent, nor even long-lasting. They generally come and go, here and there. They just happen to be in the way of you getting that special house, car, vacation or restaurant reservation. There are so many changing factors and intangibles that can suddenly influence whether the value of time, or influence will go up or down.

$$$

Shifting Obstacles and the Counter-Intuitive Process

When you develop greater skills in obstacle isolation and removal you will find that you are able to predict when a particular resource is at its highest market value. At that point you can both focus on any obstacle no matter how high or low its value may be and transcend any bottlenecks associated with that obstacle. You will also have the ability to simultaneously promote the resources with the greatest value. You will have the ability to do all of this with great accuracy, even a year in advance, since it is extremely unlikely that two or more of the Ten Cashless Currencies will have exactly the same value at the same time.

In the process of applying the many principles described in this book I discovered an interesting process for making hidden obstacles appear from behind their secret hiding places. It was one of the most exciting, and unusual ways of working with the Ten Cashless Currencies. Here is the process:

1. Observe Ten Cashless Currencies. Which one seems to have the greatest value at this time?
2. Pay attention to that one, putting the other nine on the back burner or on automatic pilot.
3. While focusing on the strongest of the ten you will notice that as the environment changes – sometimes as a direct result of the increased value of the one you have been focusing on – one of the other nine, the one

you have not paid much attention to, will begin to loom larger than the other remaining eight.

4. What you are watching is the resource with the highest value automatically rising to the top, like oil on water or cream on milk. In such an environment the strongest of the Ten Currencies becomes the most productive but with the least effort.

This is an example of what I described earlier in this section as a bird riding the thermals. It is also an example of the Chinese concept of - Wu wei and The Law of Attraction that we discussed in Section Two of this book.

Without any great action, but with your attention focused on those of the Ten Cashless Currencies with the highest value at any particular time, the obstacles will often be bypassed or simply cease to be obstacles. Why? Because they have been bypassed by alternate approaches. In those rare instances where an obstacle creates a bottleneck, you can eliminate it, transcend it or turn it into an asset.

$$$

Turning Obstacles into Assets

The turning of obstacles into assets must be done skillfully, with focus and attention to detail. It is like handling human potential dynamite, for at any time the obstacle may shift. One highly valued Non-Cash Currency may suddenly drop in value becoming an obstacle that blows up in your face while what was formerly an obstacle may increase in value and become an asset. This shift may happen without any action on your part. Market forces, or a drop in the value of the U.S dollar, or some other shift in the environment can cause this to happen.

If you have done the proper assessment and kept aware of various trends such shifts will seldom catch you by surprise. If, in this case, the worst did happen, all that has been lost is a little time. For at the end of the day all you need to do is shift your attention from one Non-Cash Currency to another. Your ability to do this is all a reflection of how much you have mastered the information and skills I have been showing you throughout this book.

Don't get frustrated if you have trouble following all of this in the beginning. Remember the end result of your mastering the process of obstacles, bottlenecks and self assessment tools is wealth and the life style that goes with it, free of the shifting values of cash, real estate or the stock market. You are cutting out the fat and collecting all the benefits of a natural, struggle-free process that is an expression of your talents.

$$$

The more you are made aware by emplying appropriate assessment tools of internal processes, the market place and your own belief systems, the more you will be able to assess accurately and beforehand which obstacle will shift. You become in a sense a futurist, for you are now able to estimate the how, why and when for any of the Ten Cashless Currencies...

- Time
- Physical energy
- Space
- Information
- Influence
- Emotional energy
- Inner wisdom
- Clarity of thought
- Dependability
- Barter of goods and services

... will change in value and how long it will take for this change to take place.

$$$

The Ten Non-Cash Currencies From Intangible to Measurable

Just to review. An obstacle is one of the ten non-cash currencies whose value has diminished so much that it is actually obstructing the process of creating wealth. A lack of time, your physical abilities, storage, living and working space, information and knowledge, influence and power, emotional energy, inner wisdom, clarity of thought, consistency and dependability, and other people's barterable goods and services can become an obstacle. The Cashless Currency that holds the highest value at that time is the one that should be used to buy what you need.

Remember! To evaluate what the cost of an obstacle will be, you must have something in mind that you want to purchase. What is the retail cash cost for this particular good or service? Now what is the obstacle that would keep you from getting this good or service at a reduced cash price or without spending the cash at all. This is the true cost. Remember, your ability to bypass the purchasing of the good or service with cash as well as your ability to eliminate the obstacles that increase the cost of buying the item will increase your available cash resources to buy those things that actually require cash – usually something that requires specificity and has urgency attached to it. Once you develop greater skills as a futurist, and observer of trends you will have the ability to track potential obstacle and their shifting value with some level of accuracy.

When you can do this your return on investment (ROI) will increase with little or no energy or cash expense on your part. You are predetermining when and where a bottleneck is going to take place before it even happens and you can bypass it.

Remember that exercise we did the chapter on Bottlenecks in Section Four, where I asked you to pour water out of a bottle? At its core, the process of obstacle isolation, valuation and removal focuses on a consistent process of increased quality of life at a lower and lower cash cost. This takes place through two simultaneous processes:

1. The direct management of obstacles that may arise.
2. The use of non-cash currencies at the very moment when they are at their highest value.

$$$

These two processes will enable you to experience a continual, rapid increase in your wealth as you manage different obstacles and profit center at the same time.

The less of your energy an obstacle requires in order to work within the cashless wealth building system the more profitable the obstacle becomes. What was formerly an obstacle becomes an asset. This new asset may even be more profitable than a superior resource that would cost more to utilize.

I have been asked. "Are you against cash? You barely seem to mention it in all this talk about trading, time, sweat equity, obstacles, bottlenecks and such." "Why not just get wealthy the normal way, like most rich people do - with cash?" My response is simple and to the point.

The truth is that few of the wealthy are wealthy because they had or have lots of cash. They had ideas, oil, software, a vision, a valuable commodity, information, influence, etc.

And I never said cash is irrelevant to this process. In fact cash is a key element in it. When the Ten cash Currencies that I have been speaking so much about are used effectively and without waste they free up cash for what cash is best used for, those things that can be purchased with cash alone. These are usually items that requires urgency and specificity - a last minute plane ticket on a specific carrier, a specific resort at a certain of year to celebrate an anniversary, etc.

By identifying those factors that have the greatest impact on the creation or elimination of an obstacle, an individual can free up cash through the conservation of the other non-cash currencies. The reduction of obstacles to free up cash and resources when they are at their highest value reduces the amount of information that must be gathered, and used in the process.

But this process creates a new issue. A person can put cash in a bank, buy CDs, stocks, or invest in something. How does one do this with a non-cash currency? How does a person store time, space or influence? That is the subject of the next chapter.

$$$

How to Store Non-Cash Wealth

So here you are, maybe not rich in the traditional sense but in possession of large amounts of time, physical abilities, storage, living and working space, information and knowledge, influence and power, emotional energy, inner wisdom, clarity of thought, consistency and dependability, and other people's barterable goods and services.

You've learned to eliminate or transcend obstacles and bottlenecks or at least turn them into assets. And you know all about balance and conservation, riding the thermals, and becoming abundant. But what do you do with these newly available resources that used to be stuck sitting in some bottleneck – particularly if they are not of use to you at this time or in the near future? It is as if you are sitting in traffic, driving a high performance sports car. Gas is being wasted, the engine is making lots of noise but the car isn't going anywhere. High performance? It's barely performing at all.

On one level it is great to have a high performance vehicle, i.e. more abundance than you can use. But on the other hand you don't want all that potential - time, information and influence to go to waste.

So what are you supposed to do with all these newly freed resources? Ultimately, to live well without cash you must discover or somehow develop a way to store these non-cash resources.

Such storage actually exists. Traditional economists call them buffers. A buffer is essentially a tool for storing all the resources that are unusable at the present time or are low in value at this time but will be valuable in the future. Buffering tools are invaluable when unexpected abundance arises.

More about buffers in the following chapter.

Creating a Buffer Bank

What you need to do is to create a Buffer Bank. Deposit some of the Non-Cash Currency with the highest value and trade a small percentage it for a large amount one of the other nine non-cash currencies that is at a lower value at this time. You might give some of your valuable time for someone else's typing ability, some of your valuable information stored in books and magazines for someone's excess storage space. The information in those books or the books themselves (if rare books) may increase in value and can be sold for cash when their value is even higher traded for something else. In reverse you might offer someone your valuable storage space, I your basement freezer to the chef who has a small restaurant with limited storage space in exchange for some of her fine gourmet cooking. And that is how a buffer bank is created. You store mine and give me yours.

When done well Wu Wei comes to play. You reduce bottlenecks and obstacles, and accumulate non-cash currency while reducing most or all of your labor. You get to sit back and read a book, watch TV, go surfing, hang glide, climb Mount Everest or if desired, just for the fun of it, even create more cash. You can do what ever you want until the accumulated, stored, resources are utilized.

Here are samples of how I create my own buffer banks.

- Buy time-shares, and fractional ownership on trade, sell them for cash on e-bay.
- Give speeches and take ski vacations in trade that I exchange for Scuba diving lessons.
- Buy a high end car – good body, lousy en-

gine – trade my friend, a mechanic, dental care for his family to store the body and find the parts - part by part – until he rebuilds it. I have plenty of time to wait for the completed car. Car value $80,000. Cost to me? Time, dental care purchased by trading on of the other cash currencies for something the dentist needed. Like money in the bank! The fun and the experience? Priceless!

$$$

Attitude is Everything

One of the three primary obstacles that we discussed earlier were Belief Based Obstacles – BBOs. These obstacles are especially important because studies have found that when a person reads comments contradictory to their beliefs, there is increased activity in several areas of the brain. These include a region involved in regulating negative emotions and another called the cingulate, which activates when the brain makes judgments about forgiveness, among other things. Also, a spike appeared in several areas known to be active when people feel relieved or rewarded. The cold reasoning regions of the cortex were relatively quiet.

In fact some people actually experience pleasurable sensations when they deny facts that contradict their core beliefs. That right! They experience pleasure denying the facts. It is common knowledge from researchers, car salesman, campaign consultants and advertising copywriters that decisions are strongly influenced by unconscious, emotional reactions. Any of us has the potential to override these biases, but you have to engage in ruthless self reflection to say, "All right, I know what I want to believe, but I have to be honest."

When a person has their emotionally-based beliefs questioned; even those beliefs that are most illogical and irrational, they may become very defensive and irate and may exhibit the brain wave changes described above. The key is not to change what one believes but their attitude about what is possible.

Believe it or not, one of the best ways to change your behavior is to change your attitudes about the object in question, in a step-by-step process of transformation. Inch by inch we must expand our sense of what is possible and our attitude about it!

Changes within a given set of assumptions happen quite easily once the learner is motivated. What is the greater motivator? A passion for something.

By identifying our beliefs, assessing them and even changing them when it is in our best interest ethically, morally and as seen through our inner wisdom, we can transform our lives for the better. By doing so we conserve resources by limiting the amount of information that must be gathered, stored and integrated into the process.

$$$

I ♡ MY
SHOPPING
CLUB

VII. SPEND LESS CASH TO SURVIVE

Spend Less Money

A commitment to spending less is not the same as being cheap! The key is to free up cash for those things that are of going to be of greatest importance. The Ten Cashless Currencies are used for things that aren't urgent so the freed up cash can be.

If spending less is done as a natural expression of your passion it will be as easy as breathing. If it is not natural for you to cut back then in time a restrained, forced and rigid approach to spending less money will soon cave in to the onslaught of impulse buying. It's all about perspective. At the end of the day a pound's worth of satisfaction to an ordinary poor man is a much greater thing than a pound's worth of satisfaction to an ordinary rich man. The rich man must often work harder to obtain satisfaction and work harder to keep it. If you are prepared to live well while reducing what you spend the first step is recycling and bare-to-the-bone thrift.

This approach will require the application of all of the Ten Non-Cash Currencies especially Information research gathering, study and application. Most of all it means not feeding your insecurities or dissatisfaction by buying unnecessary stuff. My mother, Dorothy Harrison taught me to shop smart, not cheap. She was a master at spending cash only when absolutely necessary. She told me that when she saved a dollar for essentials it was worth twice as much as an earned dollar.

When I was a kid I would watch my mother put one and five dollar bills into a collection of #10 envelopes that she kept. One envelope was marked shoes, another coat, another blouses, vacations etc. She would put 50 cents or a dollar in each of these five or six envelopes daily. Then at certain times of the year when she knew that a particular item or service would be on sale, she would buy it with the money in the envelope. Mom's envelope system was pretty basic, but it worked well. She had great style. She would take me to museums on discount days and would go to Saks Fifth Avenue, or Bergdoff Goodman's for a sale. You can recreate her system in any form you like. The key is knowing what you need and budgeting for it in a sensible way. This is what I learned from her.

$$$

Don't Shop Cheap, Shop Smart

Frugality is often confused with cheapness. Cheapness is about scarcity, while frugality is choice. It is a choice to exercise controlled fiscal restraint.

Thrift can refer to being cautious in spending, but it is really the wise management of money and resources. Remember! Every dollar in cash that you are able to save can be converted into $25-$30 worth of goods and services. That means when you take $25 in cash and buy an item that would sell for $25 at retail price but buy it instead on e-bay or at a thrift store for $10 you have saved $15. Through the application of the Harrison process – the utilization of the ten key resources at their peak value - you can convert that $15 to $300 in equivalent value.

- Think twice before spending cash for non-essentials.
- Search the Internet. Search for "frugal living" on Google or Yahoo and see what pops up.
- Collect mail order gift catalogues like Heartland America, Lillian Vernon, www.shophometrends.com, and see what gadgets you can copy or create yourself at little or no cost.
- There are a number of great books that show you how to do it in thrift. My favorites are The Tightwad Gazette books by Amy Dacyczyn, and the Hints from Heloise. You can order used copies on eBay or Amazon.com.
- Watch out for hidden fees, late charges, unannounced interest hikes, on your cell phone bill, Internet service, and the biggest culprit, credit

cards.

- Study cardholder agreements. They may allow the issuer to raise your interest rate if you pay any other creditor's bill late even if you pay their bill on time.
- Save your receipts. At the end of each month, tally the amount you spent. Isolate your most costly expenses. And figure out how you can reduce them.
- Pay your bills online. If you set up an automatic payment, you can pay the minimum on your credit card each month.
- Make cost effective beverage choices. Instead of pop, beer, wine, etc., drink water, home brewed iced tea, or plain soda water with a lime or juice.

$$$

Never Pay Retail: Join a Shopping Club

The easiest way to start reducing your cash costs is to join a shopping or warehouse club. In a addition you need to learn where there are clusters of variety and dollar stores in your area. As you become more skilled at getting more for less you will naturally branch out into thrift stores, yard sales, flea markets, swap meets, and dumpster diving. These opportunities for living rich on little cash are discussed in greater length in other areas of the book.

When you do have energy and must buy something from a traditional retailer you can still save cash by joining a shopping (warehouse) club. A shopping club is a type of retail store that usually operates in a large warehouse setting, often over 100,000 square feet in size. These stores generally sell bulk-packaged products at low prices, often at very high volume. from warehouse-style steel bins or directly off pallets. To purchase items from a Shopping Club, one must purchase a membership, usually $50 for a year or be the guest of a member. Some clubs offer a one time day pass. A 5%-10% surcharge is often added to the prices for non-members. You may also purchase Cash Cards from the stores, or shop online. to avoid the membership fee.

You can also purchase fresh produce, meat, seafood, fresh baked goods, flowers, clothing, books, software, home electronics, jewelry, art, hot tubs, and furniture, tire garages, pharmaceuticals, hearing aids, eye glasses, and much more. The discounted product and service offerings of these stores are always expanding, and in recent years, some have added investment brokers, travel agents, automobile purchasing programs where members can purchase new cars at specially arranged prices, as well as auto and home insurance. Costco is the largest shopping club chain. Others include Sam's Club and BJ's Wholesale.

Many Warehouse clubs accept only cash, and do not accept Visa or MasterCard because of high processing fees but some have changed their policies and do accept signature debit cards (no PIN necessary) and credit cards. Shopping Clubs generally offer a liberal return/refund policy in the retail business.

$$$

Go to Variety Discount Stores

Also known as known as 99 Cent, closeout, price Point or Dollar Stores, these retail stores shops sell inexpensive items, usually with a single price point for all items in the store. The first price point stores were Woolworths, Kresge and other five and dime stores, where everything cost either five or ten cents.

Though some of the modern versions of these stores call themselves dollar stores, they may have items that cost more or less than a dollar or offer some items as two or three for a dollar (and of course there is the sales tax).

These stores may specialize in certain types of goods but the best ones, more often than not, carry a combination of new merchandise and closeout merchandise bought from other stores below regular wholesale cost.

Most variety stores, especially the ones with the lowest prices are able to get access to to these great deals for four primary reasons:

1. The items are past their prime having been manufactured to coincide with the promotion of a product tie-in to a to a fast food chain or for the promotion of motion picture, television show or special event – the visit of the Pope to America in 1978.
2. The product, such as certain brands of batteries were manufactured cheaply for a foreign market but was then imported by an unauthorized distributor. These are know as gray market goods.
3. The product is packaged to look like a more

expensive brand name or is a generic version of the product. Often these discounted products are knock-offs, or have been specially manufactured for such stores – often by the same packagers who produce the more expensive brand name.

4. The product is an overstock, closeout or out of season merchandise purchased from another retail store or distributor.

Often a certain neighborhood or an area with large malls or many strip malls will have many chain or franchise dollar stores as well as thrift stores nearby. Though they specialize in ordinary products such as cleaning supplies, small tools, personal hygiene supplies, kitchen supplies, organizational supplies, small office supplies, holiday decorations, electronics supplies, gardening supplies, home decor novelties, toys, pet supplies, out of print books, DVDs and VHS tapes, food products and automotive supplies, the small privately owned, non-franchised stores can have a wide range of interesting products. I especially enjoy the ones that cater to an ethnic clientele since they will carry items I would never find in a suburban discount store that specializes in window cleaner. I once went on a road trip and found a 99 cent store that catered to an East Asian population of Indians, Pakistanis and people from Bangladesh. I loaded up on veggie burgers, frozen curry, iced green tea, Mango Lassi and soy milk.

As in warehouse stores, once you become skilled at buying what you need and avoiding impulse buys you can save a lot of cash there. Everything in a dollar store may not be a great deal since some items sold at a dollar there would have been even less elsewhere but generally speaking they are a great place to get a "bang" for your buck.

You can find many of these stores in the phone book or by "Googling" the words "99 Cent Store"

$$$

Passbooks and Coupons

There are a number of approaches to saving cash that combine barter, incentives, sales, and discount selling. Among the most popular of these are the use of passbooks and coupons. Passbooks and coupons have been a great tool for those with time, patience and good organizational skills to save lots of cash.

Specialized Passbooks: These are a money saving way to fitness. They are designed to promote many service companies, particularly gyms, health clubs, day spas, and yoga studios. A typical pass book would cost anywhere from $50 -$75 and might have as many as 325 free passes. Each pass might be good for at least 2 classes per studio, some for an entire week. The passes allow you to explore for free, many different classes anytime, anywhere and at your convenience. In NYC one such Passbook is published by The American Health & Fitness Alliance: www.health-fitness.org [212-808-0765].

Coupons - There are many ways to distribute discount coupons. They may be mailed to you for free as in the case of Val-Pak, distributed on the internet, by e-mail, by retailer or by the manufacturers of consumer packaged goods; in magazine form in popular tourist areas such as Orlando, or Las Vegas. They may be purchased in booklets containing thousands in local savings. The owner of the booklet presents a coupon to a participating business and gets a discount, usually up to 50%. Some coupons offer 2-for-1 deals at top restaurants, shops, and events and attractions. You'll may also find members-only online deals and coupons you can print right from your computer. Some booklets also offer special online shopping discounts from top retailers, hotels as well as online coupons for travel discounts and more!

To find coupon booklets in a major city check out www.entertainment.com, www.couponmom.com, or www.grocerygame.com. Basically, these booklets help you organize your coupons to match up with the sales being offered by your store. I have found it really helpful, and between that and the double coupons at my grocery store, I have been saving anywhere from 30% to 50% on our usual bill.

$$$

Price Books and Trading Stamps

Those who appreciate the concepts of saving through coupons and passbooks have created a home grown approach to getting the same or more savings - price books. With price books you are creating a formalized system for comparing prices of specific items, in specific stores and different times of the year. I have found them to be most effective when buying low price items in supermarkets and in shopping clubs but they can be created for any retail setting.

To create a price book you will need to save your grocery receipts. Using a pencil and notebook, list the items on these receipts, along with their prices. The most effective way to do this is to make columns listing the store, the price and the date.

1. Next to each entry, mark the lowest price
2. Compare this price each time you need to buy that item
3. Over several months, note each store and the specials they offer
4. Purchase enough during each sale to last until the next one

Trading Stamps are different than coupons and are especially valuable when combined with a price book system. Whereas coupons are redeemable for cash when a specific product or class of product is purchased, trading stamps act like a currency that can be traded in for certain products. The higher the number of stamps a person accumulates the more the dollar value of the goods they can trade them in for. To learn more, go to www.kingdomofbarter.com

If you are an entrepreneur there are ways of creating paper coupons: coupon books, trading stamps and non-web based forms of redemption and retail sale-based coupons that can be created without any cash through barter brokers who are experts at this process. To do this you would need to be a member of a barter brokerage exchange.

The effective use of coupons, when combined with special sales, is one of the greatest tools for reducing your cash spending.

$$$

Holiday Shopping

Here are a few ideas to keep in mind whenever you go on a shopping expedition. They are especially valuable for after holiday sales.

Make a list of what you need: This will keep you focused and help you cut back or eliminate impulse buying.

- Create price book. A well-researched price book should give you a general idea on how much a bargain price on a certain item would be. High end stores can put an item on sale at 25% off and it will still cost more then the retail price in a discount or warehouse store. Sometimes writing down what you are looking for helps focus you and also may help you stay away from items you don't want or need or can't reduce impulse purchases.

- Use your newspaper to save cash. Look in the paper the day before Thanksgiving, Christmas, Memorial Weekend, July 4, and Labor Day. Keep an eye out for coupons and special sales.

- Buy quality. Holiday sales are the best time to get higher end products at the lowest possible cost. Don't buy something because it is the cheapest. Quality lasts longer.

- Check on the store's return policy. Some sale merchandise cannot be returned or if it can it may not be returnable for cash. Learn what their return policies are and be sure you are comfortable with them.

- Ask yourself this question before you buy: If this item was full price and I could easily afford to buy it, would I? Unless the answer is a resounding yes, you may be lured to items that you won't really be happy with.

- Consider buying gifts on sale long before you need them. Buy next year's Christmas gifts the day after Christmas this year. Buy an item that you know someone would appreciate whenever you see it on sale and then store it until it is time to give the gift.

- Balance and Conserve. Sales are happening all of the time.

Don't go into debt to take advantage of sales. The interest you will have to pay may cost more than the cash you save. Wait to buy some of these items when you can afford them or buy them with one or more of the ten non-cash currencies.

Reduce Food Shopping Expenses

Food is one of the great cash expenses we incur day to day in our lives. Pre-packaged meals for home consumption, buying snacks on the run, eating in restaurants, the cost of eating out especially at social gatherings, sporting events etc. can all reduce the amount of cash you have available for the things you need. The purchasing of food is essential to survival in the way that having a car or a home entertainment system doesn't equal. When done frugally and intelligently cash savings on your food expenses can be reduced by as much as 400% - 500%. Freeing up the cash you used to spend on food for other items that can only be paid for with cash.

- Join food co-ops or shopping clubs
- Organize shopping lists
- Buy the least costly foods by unit price
- Buy in bulk
- Buy sale-priced food items that have a long shelf life
- Buy house brands
- Look for bargains in the "dented-and-scratched" basket
- Look for bargains on the lower shelves in the store.
- Don't be brand loyal or store loyal. Don't be brand loyal or store loyal
- Buy unseasoned, unsweetened packaged food – it costs less
- Avoid specialty prepared foods
- Redeem coupons on sale days

- Create a price book to compare prices from store to store
- Buy items in bulk at warehouse stores like Costco, BJs and Sam's Club
- Avoid processed or prepackaged foods made of refined ingredients like white rice, or white flour. These are low in nutritional value
- Shop fewer times per month to reduce impulse purchases
- Limit meat, chicken, or fish to special occasions.
- Use more tofu, beans, grains and vegetables.

$$$

Reduce Food Preparation Expenses

If you have free time, a food processor, a blender and the ability to pay an assistant with cash or barter to shop and do food prep for you can reduce your food costs even further.

Read the labels of commercially prepared foods and become aware of which such foods contain chemical additives and undesirable foods such as refined sugar and flour and hydrogenated oils, and gradually eliminate these foods from your diet.

Cook and freeze different foods in the same time period.

- Eat whole foods like fresh fruits and vegetables, beans, and nuts
- Eat more beans and rice
- Plan menus
- What you can use leftovers for could also be factored into your menu.
- Make different dishes from same leftovers

Grocery Saving Tips
(a free online resource for grocery shoppers)

If you think this is "thinking cheap" remember that over the course of a year, food savings alone will save you enough money for a trip to Hawaii or a week-long vacation somewhere you've always dreamt of going.

• BEANS AS A BASE FOR:

Burgers, refried beans, soups, hummus, baba ganoush, dips, Latin foods (red beans):

- Step One:

Buy a variety of beans. Split peas, lima, pinto, soy.

- Step Two:

Soak overnight in water (least expensive is Walmart Reverse Osmosis water in your own recycled plastic jar: 33 cents a gallon).

- Step Three:

Next day change the water and boil the beans until they are ready on four different burners.

- Step Four:

Freeze your beans until you are ready to use them. (Use within 6 months)

You can buy certain food in bulk and freeze it, including:

- Fresh mushrooms - Saute and freeze
- Onions,
- Cauliflower
- Broccoli.
- Homemade pita pizza with homemade sauce and freeze

The two-hour cooking frenzy: Using the food processor and working with quick cooking recipes make the following dishes for freezing.

- Refried beans
- Hummus
- Tomato Sauce
- Steamed vegetables
- Blended soups (Blanched vegetables blended with broth, vegetables or spice mix.)
- Veggie burgers

- Spice mixes - When in doubt mix onion powder, garlic powder, oregano and salt. Cayenne pepper will add spiciness.
- Seasonings can be pricey when you buy them in small packs. Instead, buy them in one-pound bags from the Atlantic Spice Co. (www.atlanticspice.com) to save up to 90 percent off the retail price. Minimum order: $30.
- Cook food by steaming or baking... By doing so you can reduce your intake of butter, fat and processed oils.

For College Students:

It's time to transcend mac and cheese, and the $1.00 Noodle packs you ate in college. Put all that stuff you learned watching The Food Channel to work. Invite four friends over for a great dinner and use plenty of exotic herbs and seasonings.

$$$

Staying Healthy on the Cheap

A healthy lifestyle includes maximizing your potential emotionally, environmentally, intellectually, physically, socially, and spiritually. Here are some tips on how to do it:

1. Create a wellness program of relaxation exercises, meditation, prayer, and good nutrition.
2. Avoid, decrease and gradually eliminate alcoholic, junk food, fast food and cigarettes.
3. Replace poor dietary habits with new healthy ones.

These are three simple rules that, if followed, invariably lead to increased health and well-being, reduced health care costs and reducing spending for food. As your overall health improves you will be less and less affected by the problems and irritations of daily life.

And when you do become ill it will be wise to familiarize yourself with simple wellness and natural healing approaches to self-health. There are many low cost alternatives to traditional medical treatments for many common problems. These remedies are safe and natural and can be purchased in health food stores and pharmacies. After all, good health is the normal human condition. Get good insurance, a solid co-pay plan or locate a barter broker who can sell you insurance on partial or full trade. Of course see a physician in any case of serious illness. When medical problems do arise purchase drugs and medications in their generic form and order and vitamins through mail order pharmacies on the Web.

No matter what your age, lifestyle, or how well you eat

- some times stuff happens: If you are having trouble paying for medications? Contact the Pharmaceutical Research and Manufacturers of America (800-762-4636; www.phrma.org). They produce a free "Directory of Prescription Drug Patient Assistance Programs." Income restrictions apply. Walmart and other large chains are offering drastic discounts on along list of pharmaceuticals.

"The proof of the pudding is not in the eating; it's in the stomach ache."

Vincent Collura

$$$

VIII. *SPEND LESS CASH TO LIVE WELL*

Clothing Chic on the Cheap

Beauty may be skin deep... But on the other hand in this fast moving world, you may only have 30 seconds to make a good impression, and good impressions can expand the value of the ten key resources.

Clothing is more than just a functional, protective covering for your torso and appendages. People wear clothing for social reasons. They are a powerful tool for cultural messages, to exude power, elegance, a sense of chic. Every article of clothing when combined with cosmetics, special scents (cologne and perfume), jewelry and other accessories and ornamentation, and many other body decorations – haircuts, coloring and tattoos contribute to and if done effectively can enhance the overall effect and message of clothing.

- Even umbrellas, purses, shoulder bags, eyeglasses and canes can add to your image. So if you are going to get your fancy clothes cheap, you might as well do it in style.
- The amount you will be able to reduce your clothing costs will depend in part upon how much of a creature of fashion you are.
- The more specific and high fashion your fashion needs are, the higher the cost will be.
- Organize your needs and budget. Know what you are looking for when you thrift shop.
- Look for sample sales and go to outlet stores.
- Other categories that are useful for buying used goods include: consignment shops, pawn shops, surplus stores, and army-navy surplus

stores.

- Adventure: Try on clothes at high end stores and then comparison shop on the web.
- Comparison shop through: msn.shopping.com, shopping.com, pricegrabber.com
- Connect to the sales staff. They can tell you about advance sales and coupons. Many large organizations give staff "friend and family coupons." If you get access to these you can save as much as 30% off of retail prices.
- Ask for discounts. If you don't ask, you don't get.

$$$

Buy Refurbished Electronic Products

Refurbished items are usually products that have been returned to the manufacturer by an individual or a store... Unlike products that have been returned directly to a store and resold by the store, refurbished goods have been examined by a trained technician at the factory and have been provided with a manufacturer's warranty. Though the warranty on a refurbished product will not be as long or inclusive as the warranty on a new product a refurbished product manufactured by a respected company should last you a long time. Refurbished items are anywhere from 10% - 25% cheaper than non-refurbished products.

Many electronics stores will resell customer returns, demonstration models and open box items at a sharp discount. Often the manufacturer's warranty applies. I've had a floor model television for twenty-one years and it still works like a charm.

Here are some tips for getting quality when buying refurbished products:

- Buy brand name products (especially brand names reviewed by consumer reports magazines).
- Avoid buying new or cutting edge products in refurbished form. Stick with technology that has been around for a few years.
- Familiarize yourself with the item. Go to a retail store, examine the product. Is it easy to use? Does it fulfill your expectations?
- If buying refurbished goods, go for a higher quality product from a reputable store. The greater

cost for quality will be worth it in the long run.

- Read the small print concerning the store's return policy. Return policies for refurbished goods are often more restrictive than for new products. Have the terms explained to you and see if you are comfortable with them.
- It's pretty easy to get refurbished items from Overstock.com.
- If you buy on E-bay, review the feedback score. If the item is to be shipped be sure that the savings are large enough and the shipping costs low enough to warrant the purchase.

Basic Recycling

When an item is no longer of use to a person, he/she may throw it out, barter it, donate it to a thrift store or sell it (pawn it). They may, if they have the time, sell the item on the internet, through dealers, at a garage sale or by placing an ad in the classified section of a newspaper. But this may not always be easy to do. It may not always be easy to find a buyer or to a dealer who can sells it for a profit. If the process takes more effort than it is worth or they may simply keep possession, dump it or donate it to a thrift store. Many department stores discard irregular goods, returned goods, products minor damages, or even perfectly functional goods that are out of style or are being replaced by newer items.

This is especially so with computers, which intrinsically have a short commercial life. Many non-profit organizations and schools cannot or will not work with used equipment even if fully functional. In the end these computers are often discarded rather than donated.

Traditionally, recycling serves the needs of the frugal, those of a fixed income, collectors, environmentalists (obtaining used goods may do less damage to the environment and reduces the amount of landfill waste) and people with unconventional tastes.

This is a boon for the individual willing to repair or use recycled stuff. This is one of the most efficient ways of conserving your cash for urgent and specific needs. It is not only culturally acceptable but is in some circles considered admirable behavior to recycle and reduce the high levels of wastage that occurs in our society. Used items can often be obtained as hand-me-downs or found for sale in thrift stores and pawnshops, auctions, garage sales, flea markets and yard (garage) sales. If you feel that buying used items is beneath you, keep this in mind. Millions of people buy houses every year that belonged to someone else first. Some houses are on their five or sixth owners! That goes for antiques, high priced art and high performance "pre-owned" automobiles as well. Would you really turn down a chance to own an original Picasso for ten bucks just because six different people owned it after Picasso? So recognize that recycling is good for the planet and if you know how to do it well it's well it's great for your cash flow as well.

$$$

Thrift Stores and Rummage Sales

A thrift store is a retail establishment operated by a charitable organization for the purpose of fundraising. Such stores are often staffed by volunteers; they generally sell used or new overstock goods donated by local for-profit businesses or members of the public who can use these donations, as they wish as a tax write-off. Because the items for sale were obtained for free, and business costs are low, the items can be sold at very low prices. After costs are paid, the remaining income from the sales is given away or used to support the organization's stated charitable purpose.

Most towns have one or two thrift stores. In larger cities there may be dozens, even hundreds... There are some areas cities that have nine or ten thrift stores in a five or six square-block area.

In such a case some, like the Goodwill Store, and the Salvation Army will have less expensive more basic items, a thermos, costume jewelry, an unopened case of pampers, some exercise contraption that was bought from a television infomercial. Right down the block will be the Housing Works Thrift Shop with high-end offerings of designer clothes and fine furniture.

There are shops I check once or twice a week. Occasionally I take a few hundred dollars and check out fifteen stores over an eight hour period, spending the day finding great deals on things I need that might have cost me thousands of dollars if bought new.

The general belief is that used items are typically worth less than the equivalent new items but this can be a misguided belief. They may be worth less than a new item purchased for cash but once you add the ten key resources what is perceived as valuable changes dramatically.

If you are polite and speak to a manager, they may be willing to lower the already discounted price on an item that has been there for a while. They may also be willing to offer you a price reduction if you are making a large purchase and ask for a discount on a specific item.

Rummage sales, known as Jumble Sales in Britain, are in a sense community organized yard sales. These sales of second hand goods are usually fundraising events organized by an institution such as a local church. usually local people are asked to donate goods, bake a cake, etc., which are set out on tables, and sold to members of the general public, who pay a fee to enter the sale.

$$$

In the last year alone I've bought an Armani suite for thirty dollars, a liquid plasma big screen television for under a thousand dollars, antique lamps, a leather Sofa, artwork, a beautiful old dresser and hundreds of DVDs and CDs. When I travel in a very hot or cold climate I will look for items that would be of value in the opposite climate. I was recently in Los Angeles where I bought an incredible designer coat, virtually new; the kind one might wear for fine dining or to wear over a tuxedo. The price? $39! Who wants a heavy coat like this in LA? Likewise I can get you a great surfboard in February in New York City. This is one of the great tricks to getting great buys in the thrift stores.

One of the limitations to shopping in thrift stores relates to mechanical and electronic products. Most thrift stores have a "buy as is" policy with electronic and mechanical items meaning you cannot return the item if it is damaged or broken. Generally the product is will be past warranty and second hand goods may be exempt from certain legal requirements and consumer protection laws. Never buy an appliances or games that you cannot test first. When testing the item make sure it works the why you expect it to. Sometimes the CD player works, but the sound is too low. The speakers are fine but the CD player isn't, etc. Consider the age of an appliance and pay attention to how well it functions and how important that particular function is to you. Many stores will allow you to return clothing for a refund or credit within a certain number of days after purchase.

The prices in many thrift stores have gone up in recent years since the demand has gone up as well. A lot of this is a reaction to e-bay and other on-line auctions. People who would never have gone to a thrift store before no go there regularly, looking for bargains that they can resell for profit on-line. Even so there are many bargains to be found.

Mastering the art of thrifting can be one of the most efficient ways of maximizing the ten key resources. In those cities with large population densities, extensive social service networks and a top layer of wealthy people who give generously to these types of charitable organizations, it can be a full time job just going from thrift shop to thrift shop finding valuable depreciated items to buy and use or resell at a higher price. Many people go to thrift stores to buy both new and used goods, or donate used items in exchange for credit towards future purchases.

$$$

Advanced Recycling: Garage and Yard Sales

Someone somewhere is moving. Someone's child has gone off to college. People get divorced, decide to have a lifestyle change, or make a decision to clean out the house. Any one of these may cause a family to set up tables and mats on the front lawn and put lots of trash and treasure out for sale. Little stickers or handwritten scraps of paper scotch taped on grandma's crystal chandelier or little Michael's Mickey Mouse Club 8-track tapes.

Garage and Yard Sales: The smallest ones (which can be the best ones) are most concentrated on holiday weekends when the kids are out of school and the family decides to take a road trip. There's cash to spend and everyone is looking for a cheap thrill. Holidays like Memorial Day, July Fourth and Labor Day bring colored paper signs stapled to light poles all over America announcing "YARD SALE, Sat. and Sun. 1/4 mile down this road, blue house on the right. 8:00 AM – 5:00 PM Rain or Shine."

If you get there at 11:00 AM, the good stuff will be gone. Many yard sales are listed in the local newspapers and Penny Savers. Those folks who are highly skilled at the science of yard sale shopping will map out a ten square mile radius, define where the wealthier areas are vs. working class are, and are up at 6:00 AM, on the road at 7:00 AM. They ready to swoop down to the front lawn of the best and biggest yard sales by 7:59 AM.

There are many great yard sale stories. One fellow bought an old picture for a few bucks and found an original copy of the Declaration of Independence hidden in the back of the frame. He kept the frame but sold the document for a few million dollars.

Flea Markets and Consignment Shops

Flea markets and swap meets are a combination of variety store, yard sale, rummage sale and 99 cent Store.

They range in size from a small corner parking lot in a large city to some in the Midwest that last for miles and consist of vendors lining the side of the road in both directions.

In NYC from Mid-March through November there are hundreds of "Street Fairs," some stretching over a mile in length and drawing over a million people. Any Friday, Saturday or Sunday you'll find them selling "dirt cheap" socks, shampoo, DVDs, laundry soap, antique furniture, toys, and overstock items from television infomercials and used and pre-owned anything and everything at very discounted prices.

One of my most interesting purchases was a collection of brand new CDs at a dollar a piece that were overstocks from the products that the Starbucks Coffee chain sells in their stores for up to $15 a piece.

Haggling – the art of negotiating with a vendor to get an item at the very lowest price possible – is a key skill in maximizing the benefits of shopping at informal venues such as garage-yard sales, flea markets and swap meets. Some individuals are uncomfortable or inexperienced in this type of negotiating situation and may choose to buy new goods on sale instead use focus on the many other approaches to saving cash that are presented throughout this program.

For the most part as in thrift stores, products bought in garage and yard sales cannot be returned if they are damaged or broken.

The key to successfully recycling other people's used stuff is of course getting a great bargain. In order to do this, you need to know what are the best times, and locations for buying specific items. In the case of thrift stores it will depend on the days and times that items are sorted and put up for sale. Occasionally, if you become friendly with the staff they may let you know when certain items come in.

On a "macro" level; reusing a used item helps society by reducing waste, protecting the environment, conserving natural resources, reduces the costly production of equivalent new goods and when purchased through thrift shops helps charitable organizations to do good works.

Consignment Selling: This is generally a profit-based dealer driven system where second-hand goods as well as some new items are offered at a lower price than retail. Consigned items may be kept in a person's home and shown to perspective customers who make appointments to see certain goods or the goods may be presented in a retail store setting. The consignment system differs from charity or thrift shops in that the original owner retains some of the profit from the sale, rather than donating it to the charity. The merchandise sold through consignment shops will include many of the same items one might find in a thrift store or at a higher end flea market. Ebay drop off stores often use the consignment model of selling.

$$$

How to Shop for Recycled Goods

I have bought boats, car stereos, paintings (created by the owner of the house), cases of suntan lotion, postcards and other collectibles. The items have great value to me because I network extensively, and a part of my networking involves making notes of the things my friends and associates collect. Old soda bottles from the 1950s, post cards from certain defunct resort hotels, obscure films, labeled Cigarette lighters from US Navy ships, Pop culture memorabilia etc. It's great for business, yes CASH BUSINESS to send someone who was a fan of the old NY Giants baseball team a gift-wrapped piece of a wooden seat from the old Polo Grounds. The cost is 50 cents plus shipping and handling. The value? Priceless! Here are some important tips on shopping at thrift stores, flea markets, garage and rummage sales.

Only thrift shop if you are going to enjoy it. Don't make it into a burden – make it into a game.

1. Act fast, be consistent and think decisively. Buy yourself a good pair of walking shoes, 'cause your gonna be moving fast on your feet. This is your job now, living well without much cash. maybe without a job. In terms of the ten key resources time is of the greatest value here since time is money and you are already saving money. Don't waste time doing it.
2. Remember you are not buying bulk items here. Each item, no matter how inexpensive, will be unique. Thrift store shopping is like a game called "Where's the Good Stuff and Who Gets

It."

3. Go often: There is a constant flux in what is available. Here today, gone tomorrow. Someone may be donating what you're looking for right after you leave the store. Plan on doing a thrift store spree once week if possible. We have a few near our home so we stop by two or three times a week. Like any type of frugal-based shopping don't make impulse buys. I know those brand new Mickey and Minnie Mouse matching toilet seats are really cute but unless you have broken two matching broken toilet seats at home pass on 'em – unless you saw someone selling them on Ebay for three hundred dollars. Train yourself to not buy unless it's really what you want or need,
4. Get knowledge about value: Some things may look cheap that are really valuable and other items look great but can be found in a 99 cent store for 99 cents. Look for damage and wear and tear when buying collectibles, ceramics, jewelry, and dishes. Know what you're looking at, read labels carefully and learn to recognize fine tailoring in shirts, suits and designer items. Used clothing can shrink or stretch and may not fit the way the size on the label would indicate. Some clothing pieces will be without tags or will only have been assigned a size by estimation. Check seams, zippers, under collars, and seams, and around button holes. If you really like the piece but it is damaged, decide if it is worth repairing. Clerks usually do not have the authority to give discounts. Ask for the manager and present good reasons for getting

a discount. Sometimes it works and sometimes it doesn't.

5. Always try on clothes when possible. In time you be so skilled that you'll be able to just look at a garment and tell if it will be a good fit.
6. Remember a pants suit labeled Georgino Armindini is not the same as Georgio Amani!
7. Take your time: Though time is of value it still must be used wisely. Budget a certain amount of time per store. You can move quickly but don't go shopping at a thrift store when you're not in the mood or you're feeling rushed. When looking for clothes deals you may end up picking through a large basket or a long rack, item by item before you find that perfect piece – and often you won't find it after all. However you may find something else very special.
8. Learn the best sale dates for different types of products, when thrift stores have special sales or auctions and when they put new items out for sale.

If necessary hire a student for minimum wage or on barter to do research on the best bargains and where to find them.

$$$

Miscellaneous Tips

This is a section made up of important money saving and money making ideas, products and services. Many of these products can be found at hoe and garden shows throughout the country.

Here are a few of my favorites, all ranging from about $10 to $30:

- Use rechargeable batteries
- PVA mops. This is a hard, foot long cylinder made from Poly Vinyl Acetate that attaches to a mop handle. Each reusable cylinder absorbs about 10 times its size in water or other spilled liquids.
- Use synthetic chamois instead of paper towels. These are highly absorbent, work better than sponges or paper towels, last longer and are cheaper in the long run. You can get about 6 of them for $20. They can be cut into smaller pieces as needed and can be thrown into the wash.
- Reduce energy costs in your home: Certain electronic appliances such as televisions and microwaves will still drain electricity when turned off, if plugged in. In combination, all of these turned off, plugged in appliances can add 10% to your electric bill. The solution? Group them all into a power strip in each room so when you go to sleep, or go on the road you can press the off switch on the power strip cutting the power off completely. This little tip can save you as much as $200 per year. Of course you

should purchase the power strip at a flea market or in a 99 -cent store.

- You can also reduce energy costs by replacing traditional incandescent light bulbs with energy saving fluorescent bulbs. The fluorescent bulbs last 10 times longer and use up to 75% less energy.
- Special pet hair removers.
- Battery operated electric can openers. They work on AA batteries, are time savers and eliminate sharp edges.
- Vacuum storage containers. These keep food fresher for days or weeks.
- Manually operated food processors, Not as sophisticated as the electric variety but this enclosed plastic shell with a turning knob and very sharp blades is safe too use and great for cutting vegetables and making mashed potatoes and salsa.
- Special patented clothes washing units that integrate the use of oxygen, ozone, and silver to eliminate the need for laundry detergent, hot water and bleach when washing your clothes.
- Fabric softening balls: These environmentally friendly specially shaped plastic balls go into the dryer as a replacement for fabric softener. They are non—toxic, and chemical free. They are great for reducing drying time, lint, wrinkles and static. They also reduce ironing time.
- Microfiber swift mops. - These can be used wet or dry for dusting and cleaning. They are reusable, easy to wash and are chemical free. A better investment than the disposable products you'd buy at a supermarket.

- Masking Tape applicator: Saves time improves accuracy.
- Antiquing: How to shop for the best for less - You can get incredible antiques and high end home furnishings in the off season in areas that cater to high end seasonal home owners as might be found in Palm Beach, Florida or the Hamptons in New York State. The Hamptons, a wealthy summer resort area along the south shore of Long Island, NY, is made up of small towns - East Hampton, South Hampton, West Hampton Beach... This area is a huge celebrity hangout – Billy Joel, Mort Zuckerman, Jerry Seinfeld, Steven Spielberg. You can get cheap hotel rooms between November and early April. Bring a couple grand with you in the winter months and go home with five dollars of value for every dollar you spend. Also check to see if these stores have outlet centers. In March-April they may move whatever has not been sold over the winter into the outlet store.
- Time is money and annoying phone calls from telemarketers waste your time and your money. To prevent those annoying interruptions call the following number from your cell phone: 888-382-1222. It is the National DO NOT CALL list. It will only take a minute of your time, and it blocks your number for five years. You must call from the cell phone number you want to have blocked. You cannot call from a different phone number.
- Free information numbers: You don't have to pay to find out somebody's number. Just call 1-800-free-411. You will be listening to some

advertisements, but would you rather be paying $2 each time you dial 411?

IX. SPEND NO CASH

Only Spend Cash When Absolutely Necessary

- Research, research and research some more to learn where the best sales are.
- Search the Internet. Search "frugal living" on your favorite search engine and see what pops up.
- Collect mail order gift catalogues like Heartland America or Lillian Vernon and see what gadgets you can copy or create yourself at little or no cost.
- Order used copies of The Tightwad Gazette books by Amy Dacyczyn, and "Hints from Heloise" books through eBay or Amazon.com.
- Watch out for hidden fees, late charges, and unannounced interest hikes on your cell phone bill, Internet service, and the biggest culprit: credit cards.
- Study cardholder agreements. They may allow the issuer to raise your interest rate if you pay any other creditor's bill late even if you pay their bill on time.
- Save your receipts. At the end of each month, tally the amount you spent. Was it worth it?
- Isolate your most costly expenses, and figure out how you can reduce them.
- Pay your bills online. If you set up an automatic payment, you can pay the minimum on your credit card each month.
- Use coupons that you receive in the mail provided you need the item. Also research coupon websites on line such as www.couponmom.com or www.grocerygame.com Basically, these sites

help you organize your coupons to match up with the sales being offered by your local store. Between that and the double coupons at my grocery store, I have been saving anywhere from 30% to 50% on my usual bill.

- Make cost effective beverage choices. Instead of soda, juice, beer, wine, etc., drink water, home-brewed iced tea, or plain soda water with a lime or juice.
- Cheap Checks. Is your bank overcharging you for check? Some charge up to $20 for a box of replacement checks. Use independent printers instead. Checks Unlimited (800-426-0822; www.checksunlimited.com), for one, charges as little as $8.95. Or try the ads in the Sunday newspaper. Have them shipped at the lowest rate. They may try to charge you some shipping and handling. It may be worth calling them to see if you can get a cheaper shipping and handling rate.

$$$

Getting Free Stuff

Once you have learned to shop at thrift stores, flea markets and other discount venues for recycled goods, you may wish to learn the art of getting free stuff. It is not something for nothing because you will still need to give back to the source of the free stuff with one of the ten key resources. You can be a good friend, an effective resource, make donations into the pool of recyclable stuff or volunteer. Here are a few of the most popular ways of getting free stuff:

Hand-Me-Downs: The most basic, easy way to obtain quality goods at low or no cost is accept hand-me-downs. These are items of some value given from the person who owns them- usually a friend, acquaintance or family member - to another who wants them at no cost. This might seem like scraping the bottom of the barrel to save a few bucks. Don't be too quick to judge. One of my business mentors, an extremely wealthy individual who is a very close friend, advisor and the best man at my wedding decided to change his entire wardrobe. I welcomed the hand-me-downs; three fine Italian suits, shoes that he had purchased for about $500 each, a ski suit, ski boots, and number of hand painted silk ties.

I was motivated to lose a few pounds so I could fit into the suits. When I wore one of these suits and shoes people I knew would come up and ask me when I had won the lottery.

Give-away shops, Freeshops: Originally started in the Netherlands this concept has spread through northern Europe and Germany and has popped up here and there in the United States. These shops, run for the most part by volunteers, are similar to thrift shops in appearance however everything there is available for the taking; is available free of charge. With the abundance of, and reduced cost of buying new technology and the increase of style-driven consumerism, there is an increase in the amount of used goods that are of little or no value to their original owners. For some people there is a stigma to taking ownership of someone else's stuff for free. Thus those who most benefit from these stores do so either by need (the unemployed poor, the working poor, students, the elderly and those carrying additional financial burdens such as single parents) , or those who would rather use their cash income more productively.

Free Market Groups: In the United States free market groups organize periodic "market days" in city parks. Participants are encouraged to share unneeded items, food, skills and talents (entertainment, haircutting, etc.), to clean up after themselves and to take home any of their own items they were unable to give away during the event. In other cases, used goods are picked up from the donor's homes thus eliminating overhead costs. Donors are often not motivated by financial need or strictly anti-capitalist conviction, but by a desire to get rid of what would otherwise be garbage without adding it to landfills.

An extension of this concept exists through the creation of the Freecycle Network. It was developed originally in Arizona for the purpose of connecting people that had extra "stuff" to get rid of and people that needed something. It is presently organized as various discussion/distribution lists, usually hosted on one of the free websites, such as Yahoo! Groups.

Dumpster Diving

Dumpster diving is a humorous term based on the image of a person diving into a large trash bin - a dumpster- for the purpose of retrieving something of value that was discarded by its previous owner.

The best Dumpster Divers sift through commercial or residential refuse usually searching for furniture, clothes or electronic parts. Dumpster divers do not actually dive into the refuse. Simply simply reaching in and pulling out what you need can access most dumpsters. In large cities like New York and Chicago, furniture that has been discarded from large buildings will be kept in the basement and put outside by the superintendent for pick up on certain times of the week. By developing a friendly relationship with the "super" you can learn what has been placed in basement for storage until the day of pickup. Certain wealthy neighborhoods are noted for having sidewalks filled with the highest quality and most valuable refuse and rejects. On evenings when pickups are made by trash collection companies you will notice people with vans fishing for fine furniture, Japanese Soji screens, air conditioners, and couches. Why not you?

Dumpster diving is great if you are a student seeking discarded things to fix for reuse in experiments, an artist looking for unusual material to create with, an interior designer looking for found items to create unique working and living environments. There have been many designers, too numerous to name, who mastered the art of dumpster diving.

Get Free Stuff and get paid to take it: A system exists where a person known as a scheduler will post job openings. The jobs include going to food stores, grocery chains, casinos, gas stations etc and any other type of retail outlet. What happen is they pay you by the job to evaluate customer service and product quality. In the case of food stores and gas stations they may pay for your food gas and groceries. They always need people.

Another company www.shadowshopper.com. organizes information from many sites and streamlines it. The down side is that they charge a small monthly fee. But if you are looking for the unique benefits offered by this service it is worth it. As always check out companies offering services on the web to guarantee that they are reputable. Go to www.violtion.com for free and look for Mr. Shopping forum.

Bartering Big Time

As you have learned in earlier chapters the most fundamental approach to living wealthy without cash is by trading your stuff for other peoples stuff. Becoming a practitioner of the art and science of trading will assist you in creating income for yourself and others that might not have existed if cash were the only option.

Trading is big business. According to estimates made by The International Reciprocal Trade Association (one of the more prominent organizations within the barter/reciprocal trade industry) more than 450,000 companies in the United States use barter and trading in their businesses. These companies produce over 10 billion dollars in annual sales. According to the United States Department of Commerce, as much as 2.2 trillion of the 10.9 trillion dollars in world commerce conducted annually is done through barter. Globally, over 480,000 businesses and six out of every ten Fortune 500 companies report engagement in barter at some level.

According to Glyn Davies in his book, A History of Money from Ancient Times to the Present, money is "anything that is widely used for making payments, and accounting for debts and credits." The type of money that is offered and accepted for payment most often - cash, coin, promissory note, check, credit card, debit card, IOU, influence, goods and services i.e., trading - will in part depend on a number of factors. These factors include how widely the form of payment is used, how easily it can be transferred, how portable it is, the flexibility of its value in times of emergency or urgency and the consistency of its store of value. When you have mastered the use of the Ten Cashless Currencies the world is your oyster. As cash is used less and less and more people become familiar with SmartCards, debit cards and a non-cash approach to doing business the skills you have learned in this book will exponentially increase your wealth, power, influence and freedom. These variables are discussed in greater depth later in this book.

As you can see, trading is many things. On a personal level, it is a simple, one-to-one barter. As a source of "cash free" wealth, it becomes a complex system that is commonly called Reciprocal Trade (RT). Whatever you want to call it, it is a path to living like a millionaire.

$$$

Practice Direct One to One Bartering

Usually direct barter results through friendships, neighborhood connections, through social connections made through religious affiliation or common interests and by researching online barter sites such as Craig's List. For direct one-to-one barter to take place there must be what economists call "a double coincidence of wants" – a situation where each person needs what the other person is willing to trade and is willing to surrender what the other person wants.

One of the ways that practitioners of the science and art of direct, one to one barter can is through hanging up flyers, using local penny saver newspapers, internet data bases, computer networks dedicated to barter and special networking websites like Craig's List' that have specific barter categories. All of these have helped expand direct one-to-one barter beyond the neighborhood. As the use of technology expands the Internet will help to create larger and more creative bartering networks. I use direct barter to get theater tickets, house cleaning services, car repairs, and more.

To maximize the potential of the web, the system of social networking, you can trade for public relations services and brand yourself as a Guru within some specialized area - wealth, wellness, wisdom, web design, graphic arts, auto-rebuilding etc. Then barter further to create linked blogs, YouTube videos, teleseminars etc. If you have the "chops" to pull it off and a strong resume to back up your claims, you can create a huge direct barter business.

One of the areas where barter is most valuable is in the exchange of goods and services that are desired but are on the low end of a person's priority list. We all have lists: A trip to Hawaii, staying at a four star hotel, or collecting fine art. Because we are using our cash for other priorities and may not wish to go into debt just so we can spend a week in Waikiki, we often deny ourselves these extra treats. Direct barter is the solution. With careful budgeting of time, good networking and the efficient use of other resources, you can accumulate enough barterable goods and services and valuable contacts to trade directly for things like that valuable piece of art we have always wanted but thought we could not afford.

Use Accrued Points and Frequent Flyer Miles

Accrued Points are units of value offered by many companies to reward customer loyalty. Typically, a person will enroll in a specific companies incentive program and then accrue points over time as they make purchases from the company or the companies partners. Accrued points can be redeemed for discounts, benefits, and free products and services.

This is one of the most information intensive approaches to living rich without cash since you have to know what company is offering what points, at what time, to whom and at what cost. Like direct trading and barter it can bring you tremendous economic freedom and help you to conserve cash.

The most popular accrued points programs are Frequent Flyer Programs offered by airlines, internet service providers, and credit card companies. Hotel chains like Hilton and Marriott also offer accrued points programs and these points may be transferred into frequent flyer miles, often at a bonus conversion rate.

You can accrue points by choosing certain cell phone carriers, credit card companies, and referring customers to certain companies. In addition many companies will let you convert Accrued Points they have issued to Accrued Points of another company.

There are many, many ways to acquire Accrued Points without actually buying the goods or services of the company giving you the point. Doing this effectively requires some time and information.

The most common way of doing this is through credit cards offered through airlines. When you use these cards you receive airline frequent flyer miles usually 1 mile per dollar spent. During certain times of the year cards may offer 2 or more points for every dollar spent. Most cards offer free, often generous up-front bonus miles for first time use.

$$$

Tips for Getting the Greatest Benefit from Accrued Points

It is becoming increasingly difficult to trade in frequent flyer miles. We tried to get plane tickets to the little Island of Malta three months before the trip and after three hours on the phone with Delta Airlines we had to take an 11 hour trip with 5 hour stops in Milan and Paris. I had the time and plenty of reading material and eats so it was OK but for most people it would have been a nightmare. A week later I booked a frequent flyer trip to Maui, Hawaii. The ticket was easy to get. All I had to do was call them 48 hours before the trip was to take place.

Accrued points become an easier and easier process, the more you master the information required to make it work to your benefit.

Remember: Read the fine print. Offers can change or expire at any time so it is important that you read the fine print. According to some experts on Accrued Points certain industries, especially telephone companies –make it a difficult and complex process to collect your points. Credit Card companies are notorious for shifting interest rates, and special deals that offer low or no interest while having plenty of hidden charges.

- Familiarize yourself with the terms and conditions of each offer for Accrued Points.
- Keep organized and detailed notes of any offer you accept for points, mileage or any other accrued points program. Be specific with dates, times, location and the person you spoke with. Call companies monthly or even a week or two after the closing date of an invoice.

- If your credit card offers frequent flyer miles for usage, check if they have a limit on the number of miles you can earn in one year. If you are going to charge a lot on a card, make note of this limit.
- Never allow a company to bill your credit card directly without first asking them if they can give you some incentive doing so. Many companies have such offers but they will not inform you of them unless you ask.
- Earn up to 1,000 miles or more from some companies by signing up for billing on line.
- Collect points by switching from one phone company top another. If their prices are high simply use less expensive phone cards, pay the minimum fees, franchise fees, network access charges, etc. and once the the miles are posted with the airline close the account.
- Get points by giving companies your e-mail address when you sign up.

Many discount stockbrokers offer generous frequent flyer miles, cash incentives or free trades, for buying through them.

One of the experts on the accumulation of Accrued Points and free offers is a fellow named Gary Steiger. He has a great website at www.freefrequentflyermiles.com. If you want to research Accrued Points, his site is one the best places to start.

$$$

Avoid Hidden Fees

Hidden fees are those fees that, though legal, are not obvious when the sales presentation is made by the service provider representative. These charges are lurking everywhere. If you aren't on the lookout, those costs can add up fast. This is particularly so concerning late fees on credit cards, going over your credit limit on credit cards, text messages, cell phones, interest rates suddenly increasing.

Businesses that are guilty of complex billing and hidden fees include hotels, wireless providers, time share resorts, fractional ownership-based accommodations, some providers of online and software tax preparation and filing services. They have been known to charge a fee to individuals who use their software and then file their tax returns electronically. Many taxpayers can use these programs and e-file their tax returns for free using the IRS Free File program, rather than the file program offered by these services. There are even credit card companies that raise interest rates to as much as 40%.

U.S. consumers collectively pay at least $216 billion in financial fees each year. That works out to about $750 a person in miscellaneous fees.

Accrued Points - Some programs have either a monthly fee or a monthly minimum purchase attached to them. Sometimes the products or services are priced higher than those of a competitor that does not offer point incentives. Some credit cards offer frequent flyer miles but with high interest rates. Make sure that the number of points you receive justify the additional fee or prices you may have to pay before accept the offer.

The solution to avoiding these hidden fees? Read the fine print on contracts and agreements or get a friend to decipher them for you.. Hidden fees a can be found in the following areas:

Your cell phone bill, Internet service provider and text message bills. According to the New York Times (March 11,2006), the worst offenders are credit card companies. Americans pay an estimated $31 billion a year in credit card fees.

$$$

INVE$T

N $

V   E

E   V

$ N

T$EVNI

X: HOW TO GET RICH

Revisiting the 10 Cashless Currencies

If you have following the program from the beginning, you will, by this point, have isolated and accumulated large amounts of the ten key resources – what were formerly nothing more than intangible assets can be converted into cash. Your contacts, reputation ideas/concepts, time, awareness, energy, dreams, desire, beliefs, enthusiasm, drive, ambition, unique background, knowledge, information, influence, experience, skills, talents, and education all have cash value.

This value, when at its peak can be traded not only for what you want or need but can also be converted into

- coins
- paper money
- negotiable securities (like a check)
- money orders,
- cashier's checks
- bank drafts
- traveler's checks
- funds on deposit with financial institutions...
- ...or invested in ways that will produce more cash.

If liquidity is what you need then cash is king! Whatever the form, cash is the most liquid form of assets. A toll for prosperity which has a fixed value and can usually be instantly. It is of greatest value when you require store of value, a unit of measure, portability, a medium of exchange, urgency and immediacy, a general instrument of power and prestige, fungibility. With the skills you are soon to develop you will be able to trade cash for the Ten

Cashless Currencies and convert them back into cash choosing which to use and when based on your needs and the value of each.

An example of this was my recent trip to Europe. The value of the U.S dollar had recently had a dramatic drop in relation to the Euro. We conserved our cash and did plenty of trading on the trip, saving a considerable amount of cash.

Manifesting Wealth

Everything in life involves change. Everything passes from one state to another, varies in form or essence and is altered so that it may even change to a form that is virtually unrecognizable from it's former existence. Time makes things different from what they were; or substitutes one thing for another. We undergo variation, are partially or wholly transformed, and pass from one phase to another. Seeing that this is true, it is madness to act as if life is anything but change and transformation. In this chapter you will learn to transform ordinary thinking about cash, money and wealth into total abundance thinking.

Success happens at the very moment that preparation and an opportunity meet. When a person is ready, willing and able, all manner of unforeseen events and circumstances arise to support them in the fulfillment of their vision, without actual planning discipline or willpower at the moment of fruition. It is all a process. The very thing you wanted was always there. You were just looking in the wrong direction.

You can actually experience this by practicing the following simple exercise.

1. Close your eyes and pick a color in your mind, any color.
2. Now open your eyes and carefully look around the room for the color you have chosen. Look at the details of the room for the color– pictures, chair legs, trimmings, accessories, etc. I'm sure you now see this color all over the place.

Did you notice this color in the room before you did this exercise? Probably not! The point is, that it was there all the time. But your attention wasn't on it.

When you are ready to have an economically abundant, struggle free life, it will happen. This is not some motivational, inspirational hocus pocus. This is how things happen, with love, passion and wealth. It is the unfolding of natural law. Its already happening. You're simply looking in another direction so you don't see it.

$$$

Investing

The individual who does not know the difference between these three ways of handling money is bound to end up in poverty. It would seem, after all, that the term "investment" would be easy to define, but in fact it is used differently by different types of experts. For instance an economist would speak of an investment as a real investment such as a machine or a house. Financial economists on the other hand refer to financial assets, when money is put into the stock market, securities or other monetary or paper (financial) assets in the money markets or capital markets, bonds, or in fairly liquid real assets, such as gold, real estate, or collectibles which may then be used at a later time to buy a real assets. The method for assessing whether a potential investment is worth its price is known as valuation.

When people say to me "good luck" I enjoy responding, "you know what they say? The smarter you are the luckier you get!"

Though banks often call a savings account an investment, this is inaccurate. This distinction is important, as investment risk can cause a capital loss when an investment is realized, unlike savings where the monetary value is influenced by inflation but will not fluctuate the way true investment value would fluctuate.

Being smart in your financial affairs means using influence, information and times to make investment decisions. This approach is less riskier than speculation or gambling.

Once a person decides to invest they have to become clear what their long term and short-term priorities are? This is important since the value of an investment may not be clear for some time whereas the outcome of a wager is evident within a short period of time.,.

Remember: Investing in anything, especially the stock market, involves risk. Investing by it's very nature creates gains and losses. You have to be successful enough to produce gains that not only overcome losses but also overcome; taxes, fees and inflation and the cost of paying back your debts if you have any and the interest costs on those debts as well.

$$$

Speculating and Gambling

Though investments in instruments such as stocks, bonds and real estate are usually not considered gambling, they can involve significant risk if not done intelligently. Unless you are a full time or "professional investor" you will more often than not make investments indirectly through intermediaries, such as insurance companies, investment clubs, banks, mutual funds, and collective investment schemes. Even so, wise investing requires that you require more information than you might speculating or gambling.

Speculators lie somewhere between gamblers and investors. For though they have more information to make decisions with than a gambler would, they still must anticipate increases or decreases in a particular market value. The good news is that unlike gamblers, speculators may be able to influence the market place through their investments. It is their capital that is needed to facilitate the liquidity.

Gambling - the act of playing for stakes in the hope of winning- is the very antithesis of this. It is virtually always an an event with an uncertain outcome. We all make poor or ill-advised choices in our lives. On close observation it is clear that and there is no choice that one can make that is more irresponsible than gambling with your financial future.

Gamblers are risking their money on an idea with too many uncontrollable variables. A professional gambler is really a speculator because they have the ability to make judgments on some of these variables. Obviously a very skilled professional gambler can create wealth.

There are very, very few skilled professional gamblers and if you are not one of them do yourself a favor and stay away.

$$$

Become a Barter Broker

Anyone can become a barter broker. The cost is low and if you are a good networker, rich in information and with basic entrepreneurial skills you will do well. The most successful barter brokers produce large amounts of cash income through initiation fees, transaction fees and monthly charges to their members. Best of all they get first choice on buying the most valuable goods and services since they have access to many brokers throughout the world and become aware of what is available for barter company members do.

A barter business is not a license to print money. You must keep good records, pay taxes on barter profits and provide what their members need or you'll soon go out of business. If you decide to become a barter broker you will want to develop effective networking templates, learn accepted industry-wide ethical standards, and stay aware of governmental policies and actions that affect the barter industry. As a barter broker you will have exclusive contacts, suppliers, obscure barter currencies, relationships with small independent brokers in the middle of nowhere and more. The easy way to accomplish all this is to join an association of barter brokers. Still you can maintain your membership as a retail customer of some of the larger barter exchanges while building your company.

The most influential of the barter associations and trading groups are:

- The International Reciprocal Trade Association (IRTA)
- web: http://www.irta.com
- The National Association of Trade Exchanges (NATA)

- http://www.nate.org/
- http://dobarter (Do Barter Network)
- swapthing.com (Free)
- barteryourservices.com
- U-exchange.com (Free)

I am a Barter Exchange owner. You can join my organization by going to www.kingdomofbarter.com

$$$

XI: HOW TO CREATE MORE CASH

Why Cash is Sometimes Easier to Use than Barter

If you need something right now and in a certain form there is no better way to get it than with cash. Cash is the greatest tool of commerce for the individual who requires short-term gratification, immediacy and specificity in their business dealings. Of course, unless you are hungry for a certain type of candy bar, these qualities are not the most desirable. Those who live in psychologically driven universe of "I want, now and my way," tend to end up slugging it out in zero sum games with others who are driven by the same motivations they are. In addition to this cash of course does have it's own inherent problems. It has to be stored, insured, protected and you can't even control or manipulate its value. This is the job of the Federal Reserve Bank and the SEC –The Securities and Exchange Commission.

Cash is more vulnerable to theft than most barterable goods and services. Cash is also a greater draw for criminal activity because it is usually untraceable. This is why cash is the medium of choice for those involved with bribery, counterfeiting, tax evasion, money laundering, extortion, kidnapping and other criminal activity.

That being said I am a fan of cash when it is used for those things it serves best:

- A more constant means of measurement - it's acceptable in many situations and cross culturally.

- Portability - You can carry money around more easily than a camel, or twelve loaves of bread.
- Store of value. Cows can die. Money can't. You can transfer money into tax-free municipal bonds. It's virtually impossible to do that with an apple pie no matter how good the apple pie is.

The point here is that cash is not good or bad. It is just one more resource to be used and leveraged against all of the ten cashless currencies for the purpose of giving you a passion filled life filled with leisure and economic independence.

$$$

Four Factors to Creating More Cash

Once you decide that a certain situation requires urgency and specificity than you must convert your non-cash currency resources into cash. The more effective you are at concerting one dollar of time, space or information or influence into one dollar of cash, the wealthier you will become.

INSIGHT

It is necessary to assess the amount of non-cash currencies you have available to you as well as the skills and strengths that you possess. Now and look at ways to market them.

INVESTMENT

Investment is an extension of commitment. Energy cannot be destroyed, it only changes its form. Every thing in life is a cause or an effect. When you effectively invest cash or time, money, resources, belief, etc. you will receive results that are much greater than your initial investment.

COMMERCE

There is no such thing as a "FREE LUNCH." Every opportunity requires time, effort, barter, money or a combination of these four factors. Know what you are worth in the marketplace and take your investment there.

PATIENCE

After you have accomplished insight, investment and commerce then it is time to sit back and wait. Let time your actions, and commitments come together. There is a time element that can be frustrating if you are insecure, have a lack of vision or have a shortage of faith and hope. THIS APPROACH DOES WORK!! The majority of my mentors say you must allow 20 to 90 days. "ALL THINGS COME TO THOSE WHO WAIT."

Remember! Increase your income while reducing your expenses. Evaluate all areas of your economic life. Select an area in which you believe you can increase your cash income and do so.

Remember, save cash for times where urgency and specificity are required. Your friends may call you "cheap" but at least you'll be scuba diving in Hawaii while they're calling you cheap.

$$$

Buy and Sell at Auction

An auction is the process of buying and selling goods, services, idea and information by offering them up for bid, taking these bids, and then selling the item to the highest bidder.

An auction, in the purest sense, is a method for determining the value of a commodity when that commodity has a fluctuating or undetermined price.

Most of us have been exposed to what is called a standard auction. This is the type of auction you will usually see in a movie or television show. In this type of auction someone makes a bid of a certain amount for an item. Once this bid is made, the initial bidder may get the item unless others bid a higher amount that is what usually happens. As bidders increase the selling price of the item the price will continue to rise until the bidding peaks. When there are no longer any bids the highest bidder gets the item.

Certain items at a standard auction will have a minimum starting bid – a "reserve price". This is a secret minimum amount the auctioneer may accept as the final bid. When the reserve price is not met the auctioneer has the freedom at the conclusion of the bidding to not to sell the item at the closing price. In an auction with a reserve price the person who puts the item up for auction may owe a fee to the auctioneer or auction company even if the item is not sold. In auctions where there is no reserve price, the sale is guaranteed. The price at which the item will be sold is left to be determined at the auctions end.

Any thing can be auctioned, including barter items offered through auction can come from anywhere but many of the finest goods sold at public auctions consists of property liquidated in bankruptcy, seized by the IRS, customs or are part of estate sales – often the remaining property of people who have passed away. Major auction houses such as Christie's, Sotheby's, produce and distribute catalogs of rare and/or collectible items.

There are many types of auctions. Each offers a unique approach to how goods are presented, minimum prices are set, and the bidding process. The finer auction will offer catalogs of what is to be auctioned. Some of the catalogues themselves may be elaborate works, with extensive information and details about the items being auctioned.

Types of Auctions:

Look up auctions on the web by going to a search engine and typing in the subject space "What is a —" and putting in the name of the type of auction you want to learn about. Some of the most common types of auction are: The Absolute auction, All-pay auction, Buy-out auction, Combinatorial auction, Digital art auction, Dutch auction, English auction, and so on...

Ways to make lots of money or at least live as the rich do through auctions include:

- Purchasing goods at an online auction or thrift store and reselling them at a high end auction
- Developing knowledge of art, fine rugs, or furniture and getting valuable items at steeply reduced prices. That can be traded for things of greater value or sold at a higher price.

Internet auctions: These are an online service where users can list goods for sale and bid for items. Ebay is the most well known of the internet auction companies, In an internet auction you are buying from private individual than from the site. Buyers don't have as many rights in a private sale then they would at a public auction.

Before the sale takes place an on-line auction site should list what protection you have. You will find this usually published in the terms and conditions section on the auctioneer's website. So review the site out carefully, before you sign up. Many, sites encourage feedback from buyers and sellers, so that you can review out the comments posted by other users before you commit.

If you are buying items through online auctions you have to have patience. It sometimes takes months to find specialized items at a low price and new postal rules have increased the cost of shipping. Still if you know what you are doing you can get great deals here.

The best way to become proficient at auction buying and selling is to attend a number of standard, public auctions and observe the goings on carefully. Then bid on inexpensive items you might like. The easiest way to find these auctions is to look in classified adds of the business section of the newspaper.

Barter Auctions: A popular system for expanding the value of what you have, and the one that for the most part does not require some amount of cash is the Barter Auction. This is a specialized form of auction where bidders can offer virtually anything as payment, including barter credits from different exchanges or some other product/ service in exchange for the auction product/service.

There are many types of auctions and Barter Auctions have many unique qualities not associated with traditional auctions.

Of the many types of auctions that exist, a Barter Auction is most similar to the standard auction. One difference between a Barter Auction, also known as a Trade

Auction or Exchange Auction is that in most types of auctioning, the highest bid wins. Barter Auctions works very differently from other auction types, in that the auctioneer does not automatically choose the winning bid. In a Barter Auction, the auctioneer determines which bid, if any, is acceptable in exchange for the item being auctioned. In this way, the auctioneer has the freedom to accept whatever offer he or she chooses. This may include specific products and services or combinations of different products and services in lieu of a cash payment.

Barter Auctions may be privately sponsored and include offerings and bids from anyone with something of value to sell or anyone willing to make an offer or trade for other goods or services. Anyone can participate, even if they aren't a member of a barter exchange company. Many real estate brokers and agents, creative business owners, barter exchange brokers, trade club members and independent traders attend Barter Auctions.

Even if you do not belong to a trade exchange or do not know any barter brokers, you can create your own barter auction. Call friends and associates and invite them to participate. Each person pays a simple cash fee. Supply refreshments and spend a great evening bidding on various goods and services. It is a great networking tool and is an entertaining way to save cash and get what you need.

$$$

XII: BUILDING WEALTH WITH THE CASH YOU'VE CREATED

Creating Wealth with the Cash You Have

We have already discussed that, however you choose to invest, it is best to get what you need without cash when possible. This process allows you to free up cash and will enable you to invest it or use it for some special treat that will greatly enhance your quality of life – a special treat that might only be obtained with cash. You can even use the cash to pay your back taxes, utility bills, or you can store it in a savings account as an emergency fund – to be used when you actually require urgency and specificity.

In the old days, people became wealthy doing one thing – drilling for oil, manufacturing a product, franchising etc. Nowadays, with ever greater technology and greater opportunities for all of us, no matter who we are and what our beginnings, many individuals have become wealthy by creating semi-passive, multiple streams of income. These are business vehicles that have steady annual growth, high return on invested capital, generous cash flow, and offer long-term prospects for continual expansion.

Here are some approaches to creating passive income streams:

- Buy and sell on Ebay
- Start a home-based travel business
- Network marketing
- Become a barter broker

- Become an agent for others and create business through networking
- Real Estate
- Collect art
- The stock market
- Sell information on the Internet
- Invest your sweat equity in someone else's business

Investing in Credit

A unique way to create a cash profit from OPM (Other People's Money) is to invest with your own credit line credit. Investing in credit is a risky process and should only be done by those who are immune to ordinary greed and short-term gratification. It is not the best way to create cash but it is not as risky as speculating or gambling. When you are investing in credit you are borrowing as much as you can, as fast as you can, and reinvesting it. If you do this irresponsibly it can lead you to financial ruin. The goal is get a greater return on investment than the cost of the interest on the credit you are investing. Do not use credit to cover day-to-day expenses. The amount you invest and what you invest it in will change from decade to decade depending on the changing market environments. In the nineteen seventies people invested in such items as trust funds and art. Inflation and tax write-offs made it more than worthwhile. Even if you don't need the money, you can borrow just to get in the habit. It is key that you borrow sanely and not put yourself in a range beyond your ability to pay back what is owed. If you are earning $15,000 monthly you might be able to borrow $10,000 right off the bat.

Here are some guidelines for investing your cash profits from investing in credit:

- Contact a financial planner and look at investment opportunities
- Investigate how you can save on taxes.
- Contact a financial planner
- Study ways to save on taxes
- Create a household budget.

- Track debts and pay them down by consolidating loans.
- Track expenses using software, such as an Excel spreadsheet
- Organize your receipts in a simple file and total them up each month.

$$$

Use Third-Person Barter and Professional Barter Brokers

Once you have experienced how your quality of life has increased through the use of barter you may feel the need to expand beyond basic direct one-to-one barter. It is at this point where you may want to learn more about professional barter brokers and larger third party Barter Exchange Companies.

A barter broker is a third party that creates barter arrangements between two or more individuals or organizations looking to do business.

Once you go beyond direct barter you will need to join what is commonly called a Reciprocal Trade Exchange. Reciprocal Exchange companies – generally called barter exchanges - are associations of different professional and retail merchants who barter surplus goods and services. The Barter Companies may charge an initiation fee, membership fee, monthly charges and a percentage of the barter transaction. Unless you have a large network of your own it is difficult to save cash and build your use of barter on a substantial level without the support of a barter broker. So many Americans engage in barter using brokers that some barter broker networks do hundreds of millions of dollars of business annually. The best barter brokers monitor prices and prevent overcharging thus maintaining the value of the trade dollars they have issued.

Barter/RT Exchange Companies are so creative and entrepreneurial in the development of ever more effective, ethical, "out of the box" business models for creating wealth without cash, that many of these small companies have gone beyond the basic record-keeper model. These exchanges have evolved into a combination clearinghouse, lead generator, third party record keeper, stock exchange, alternative financier, bank/ brokerage/ investment company, securities business, and classified advertiser.

There are some small barter/RT organizations with single offices and some very large barter companies with over a hundred offices throughout the world. Some larger barter companies combine the benefits of the local barter exchange with a national network by franchising offices in local areas and connecting these individual offices through a national office. The downside is, that the strength of a local office is defined by the talents, and abilities of the person running the office. This can lead to strong offices in some areas and very weak offices with poor customer service in others.

Some individuals, businesses and some barter companies who are valued in the barter community create their own negotiable currency. In the barter industry this currency is known as "scrip". This scrip, is usually purchased in specific, minimum denominations and may even look somewhat like money. Scrip can be used to purchase products or services from anyone who will accept the scrip.

This is how a retail barter broker works. When you use a barter broker A no longer need trade with B or even know of Bs existence. Both A and B have the freedom and are likely to trade into and out of the barter brokers network. Members (clients) of Barter Exchange companies use barter credits (trade dollars) instead of cash to conduct transactions. Trade dollars are the accounting units of barter exchange companies. Trade Dollars may exist as actual printed, "trade money" or as a computerized record with e-mails and a paper trail attesting to what is in the individuals account. Trade dollars are sometimes superior to cash because they are impossible to counterfeit, and can be used as an electronic currency in exchange for goods and services, something that cash can not be applied to.

If a member trades $1,000 worth of products to another member, he/she gets other products or services available in the exchange. Instead of receiving cash the company receives barter credit with the trade exchange. The exchange maintains a diverse catalog of goods and services for which its clients can redeem their barter credits over time.

Internet Riches

One of the key vehicles for creating cash and non-cash wealth is through the Internet. If you are not internet savvy, learning to use this valuable tool for information and commerce is essential.

The Internet is a collection of approximately 60,000 independent, inter-connected electronic networks. These networks are connected primarily through phone lines, and wireless technology, the same type of technology used in a cell phone. The networks in turn link disparate computers and systems. Virtually every university, government, and research facility in the world and millions of commercial sites are on the Internet. In order to process, utilize or selling of information you must become familiar with the internet, and how to utilize the most popular web-based resources - Google, Yahoo, Amazon.com, and Ebay as well as their competitors. It can all be learned step by step, easily and you don't have to own a computer to do it. Use library computers for free or use low cost Internet cafés. In fact the Internet has hundreds of millions of users worldwide, and that number is growing rapidly. Over a 100 countries are linked into exchanges of data, news, blogs, video networks, on line radio and television.

Most of the Internet or as it is commonly called "the web" consists of the contents of thousands of specialized searchable databases that lead to websites. When you type a search in one of these databases, such as "auctions" or "discount plane tickets" the search results are delivered to you by listing web pages that are a direct response to your search. You open the sites, research what you need and "bookmark" it – make a note of it on your computer for future reference.

You can make millions and save millions through the internet in the following ways:

- Offering goods and services for sale through your website including on line-seminars, coaching, e-books, and newsletters, as well as affiliate programs and on-line partnerships
- Auction sites through which you can advertise and sell goods
- Link with other host sites that provide a venue for to advertise and sell goods.
- Networking to create income - People who are skilled at using the internet use the same skills one might use on social-networking sites – making business contacts, meeting trading partners, posting profiles and emailing trade offers back and forth and even calling each other to create long term strategic relationships.

$$$

In his book "Why Things Bite Back: technology and the Revenge of Unintended Consequences," Edward Tenner draws many examples from daily life of how complex our lives have become, though we have created technology to make it all easier. People used to go to the bank in the daytime to complete their transactions. Technology gave us cash machines so that we can use a plastic card and a code number to extract money after banking hours. Even so studies have shown that the lines are longer now in the evening at cash machines than the lines we used to wait on during normal banking hours. He points out that before safety equipment was developed for aggressive sports, people were forced to be careful in order to avoid injury. In recent years more sophisticated helmets and other protective gear have made sports technically safer and yet there are more injuries than ever. Safer equipment, it seems, has lead athletes of all types to take greater risks. Why? Because people become more reckless in their sporting behavior due to the sense of security they have with this equipment.

It was believed by many that the advent of the personal computer would provide great benefits with little or no negative effect. Bu the computer has requiring workers throughout society to discard their previous skills for those required to effectively use computers. Now all types of new medical problems have arisen from people sitting in chairs, repeating the same motions over and over and staring into the computer screen. Back problems, hand and arm problems and vision problems are the result.

It is the way of humans to create change or improve things wherever possible. This applies to technology as well as man's relationship with his natural surroundings. Many of these attempts at improvement, though done with good intentions often go awry. Mr. Tenner points out, that new forms of transportation like airplanes, trains and automobiles have unintentionally allowed viruses, insects and other various animals to migrate from their natural habitats to new regions causing destruction and havoc to the new ecosystems. The point? Avoid unnecessary complexity.

Certainly technology has changed how we live our lives, but not without a great cost. Achieving contentment and economic freedom requires more than buying the next technological advancement. It requires greater inner knowledge of our wants, versus our needs. Simplicity comes easily when you have a vision or mission in your life.

Start Your Own Business

When you work for someone else you will always be paid less then your time is worth. That's just how it is. The owner hires you to produce a good or service and pays you less then they can sell it for. The difference between your salary and benefits and the price your employer sells the product or service for is their profit. If they paid you what your time was worth they would not be making a profit.

Of course one of the benefits of working for someone else is the sense of security a job provides. On the other hand you can always get laid off and unless you are a great salesperson working for commission or a brain surgeon you will never get rich working for someone else!

When you own your own business you have essentially taken the step to take charge of your economic destiny. One of the greatest obstacles to building your own business is simply the cash cost of getting started. The Living Rich System is perfect for the budding entrepreneur.

Remember - Goods and services traded directly, like cash, are forms of money. They are simply not as consistent in their benefits as cash. If you are starting a new business, you can negotiate for lower rent, and avoid a high initial cost outlay by taking a raw space rather than a fully renovated space. You may need to collect favors owed to you or trade your services directly for the space rental. If you lack what the owner desires, you can bring in your own workers and pay them with what they need for customized improvements like painting, installing dry wall, plumbing and electrician services, all paid for without cash..

Combining barter with cash in your business gives you a competitive edge that purely cash based businesses lack. Those clients, interested in using barter will bypass purely cash based businesses to do business at an establishment that accepts barter while keeping their existing cash clients. In addition to this, barter for the most part is less fad driven than cash. Fad driven goods and services are usually purchased with cash since immediate gratification is generally involved in such purchases. Clearly cash is more desirable when buying and selling almost anything related to immediate gratification. But any purchase that is not an "impulse buy" will be perfectly suited to barter.

Here are the basic areas you will need to learn about to start your own business:

- Determine the type of business you wish to create: a product-based business with a retail location; a service business, an e-commerce business
- Determine how much you will need to pay yourself from the very beginning once you decide to start your own business
- Research your business idea
- Create a business plan including a marketing plan
- Determine which Business Licenses and Permits will be required
- Find a great location for your business
- Hire an attorney through barter to handle key legal issues
- Determine if and what you need to Name Your Business
- Create a logo
- Create a great business card
- Find product sources

- What should you charge?

Reduce risk in your business adventures: A "risk" is the expectation that a threat may succeed and the potential damage that can occur.

Here are some tips for reducing risk. If the choice you make requires or can result in any of the following then the cost may be too high:

- Lawsuits, fines, or imprisonment
- You need permission and haven't asked for it
- The act may cause you extreme public humiliation
- It's immoral
- It will serve you but at someone else's expense
- It will put you deeply in debt
- Creates unnecessary struggle in your life
- Disconnects you from your passion

Direct Selling as a Path to Wealth

Direct selling, also known as multi-level or network marketing is big business. It generates over over $100 billion dollars worldwide and has experienced almost a hundred percent growth between 1996 - 2006. A person in the direct selling business has the opportunity to become financially independent without employees, payroll, upfront investments, office or storefront rent, or investment in merchandise. If done effectively, it is a business with unlimited possibilities and mass appeal – perfect for a person who has mastered the ten non-cash currencies.

Direct selling is based on the concept that networking and word of mouth recommendations is the fastest and most cost effective way to market a product or service. Direct selling companies offer an individual the opportunity to experience a product or service and receive compensation for recommending the product or service to others. This compensation expands so that they also can receive cash payment when those they have recommended the product or service to recommend it to others as well. In time one individual can create links of hundreds, even thousands of distributors or associates in long networks known as down-lines. This business allows them to delegate almost all of their labors to others and receive residual income– income that continues producing long after the work that created it has been completed. A traditional start-up business or franchise usually requires a sizable investment. A person who gets in involved with a direct selling usually purchases it as a kit for about $25 to $100. This kit includes manuals, instructions, company policies and procedures as well as product information.

Companies such as Lillian Vernon, Timer Warner, Citigroup and Richard Branson's Virgin Cosmetics Company are all involved in the direct selling industry and Robert Kiyoski, author of the Rich Dad, Poor Dad Series as well as Steven Covey, the author of "7 Habits of Highly Effective People" have each commented on the benefits of direct selling for creating wealth.

To do well in the direct selling business it helps to be social and friendly with good networking and follow-up skills. Look for products and services that are exclusive to the company you are distributing for. Choose products that are not easily available through other venues. Concerning direct selling, billionaire Warren Buffet stated: "The best investment I ever made."

XIII: SLEEP CHEAP AWAY FROM HOME

Learn to Travel on the Cheap

Millionaires tend to travel a lot both for vacation and business. For the street smart person travel is seldom decided by the state of their finances since you can travel by car, bus, train and plane, and the quality of each experience will be different based on your life style needs. Here is a cornucopia of travel tips and strategies.

- Take the bus. if you have the time it's the most economical way to go. Bring food, a cassette player, a DVD player and you're set. Bus fares will vary. You don't have to go with the big bus companies like Trailways, or Greyhound. There are many bus companies that service specific ethnic or religious groups like Chinese, Orthodox Jews or Evangelical Christians. If you are comfortable with different types of people this is a great way to go. In NYC there is a bus that goes to from Chinatown to Boston for $15. that is half the price of the "brand" name bus companies. You can find these on the internet or just by networking.
- Transporting cars: There are people who need to transport their cars from one city to another and can't do it themselves. They don't want to pay to ship the car either. If you have a clean driving record and good references you can drive their and they'll pay for your gas. This is sweat equity and it costs you nothing but time.

- Get an RV: You can reduce the cost of both travel and hotels by buying or renting an RV (Recreational Vehicle). This is especially economical in the Southwest and in Florida where there are many dealers of such vehicles. There are even Barter Brokers who can do this for you.
- Find resources for travel discounts such as Arthur Frommer's Budget Travel Magazine, go to biddingfortravel.com, or go to specialized internet bulletin boards such as www.flyertalk.com
- Get paid to travel: Have you considered a career as a Tour Professional. There are dozens of jobs available in the travel and tourism industry. You can get low or no cost training. You can work as an independent contractor get great pay and see the world. There are Tour Operators looking for bright, informed and articulate people to take student and adult tours in the USA and throughout the world.
- Fractional ownership of a plane or air-time: Even the rich deserve break. If you fly over 300 hours a year consider sharing the cost of a plane as a group purchase. If you fly a lot consider fractional ownership of a plane. This is essentially a time-share but rather than owning time in a hotel or resort you are buying a set amount of flying time. Some of the more successful enterprises selling fractional air-time include AvantAir, Flexjet, and Flight Options.
- Most airports rent out a luggage cart at the baggage claim area from $3 -$5. Bypass this cost by going to the taxi pick up area for a luggage

cart that someone else has used and left empty.

- Beware of all-inclusive trips. They are not always the most cost effective approach to travel unless you use all the amenities, eat three meals a day and consume plenty of drinks. Compare the all inclusive fee with what the cost would be without that option.

Reduce the cost of exchanging currency when traveling. Here are some tips:

Use your debit or ATM card to withdraw money from an ATM as soon as you arrive. European banks almost always charge lower rates than commercial exchange counters.

Do as few exchanges as possible since you will be charged each time for processing, servicing and administrative fees.

Travelers checks are good and AMEX has a reloadable Travelers Check card. This card requires a minimum $300 deposit and gives you a max. balance of $2,700 to work with. It can, however, be replaced if lost and is not connected to your bank account or any credit cards. These are not the best choice if you will be in a remote location. You can buy the funds in dollars, Euro and pounds.

For inexpensive European Hotels go to www.eurocheapo.com Neotravel.com, TravelSense.com Some of these will even give you discount coupons of future purchases associated with travel.

Save on Airfares

Airfare is one of the most costly investments in long distance travel and yet if people use the right information at the appropriate time, they can save lots of cash and possibly even get paid to fly. This chapter offer a cornucopia of approaches to getting where you are going with tips on where to find the best deals on cheap airfare and the best time to purchase tickets, how to get frequent flyer miles and the best times to use them, what travel agents to seek out, what websites for buying tickets have the lowest or no hidden charges, and much more.

Cheap airfare: There are a few basic tips that anyone can apply with ease including:

- Avoid peak travel days – Those before and after an actual holiday. Look for flights two days before or after a peak or holiday period. Sometimes you can save by flying on a holiday when most people would rather be home. Flying on Xmas or New Years Day is always less expensive that just before of after the holidays. Compare airfares on the web and sign up for e-mail newsletters that will inform of sales and special packages. You can also become an air courier (more on this in the next chapter).
- Buy tickets over the Internet.
- Only use freq. flyer mile on trips out of the US or Hawaii to get the best return on investment.
- Fly between September and Thanksgiving
- Don't book flights earlier than 150 days in advance or more than 14 days in advance. Generally airlines don't offer discounts or sales

during these time periods.

- Split Ticketing - Travel agents in one country can issue tickets in another, taking advantage of differences in price at one end of a route. This facilitates "Split Ticketing" whereby you can save by combining two one way fares for a round trip, especially in first class or business class.
- If you travel frequently to a particular place, it's often cheaper to book a one-way ticket (or a discounted round trip) to that destination, then book a series of round trips from there. This is especially true in Bangkok."
- Cheap flights in Asia: If you are flying to Asia consider starting in Bangkok, Thailand. If you buy plane tickets you can get steep discounts to other locations.
- If you are flying to a certain country, explore travel agents in neighborhoods that have a large population of individuals from that country. An agent in Astoria, Queens may get special discounts for tickets to Greece, Columbia or Bangladesh.
- If you already booked a flight and it is cheaper later on, you may be able to call and explain the situation and get the cheaper price.
- Cheap-Caribbean.com
- Look for deals on-line for labor day travel.
- Call late for the best fares. The best airline fares typically go to those who call just after midnight, East Coast time. That's when airlines decide whether a flight is full and begin slashing prices if it's not. Fares can drop by anywhere from $50 to $400.

Among the most popular web sites that can be researched for low cost fares and general travel tips are:

- SmarterTravel.com
- Travelzoo.com
- Cheapflights.com
- Airfarewatchdog.com
- Priceline.com.
- TravelSense.com
- Neotravel.com
- Kayak.com
- Sidestep.com
- Mobisimo.com

$$$

Travel for Next to Nothing by Becoming an Air Courier

A courier is a person who delivers something for someone. People who deliver cars for others are a type of courier. An air courier is a specialized type of courier – an individual who acts as an agent simply by occupying a seat on a plane. This courier permits a courier company to transport time sensitive packages by air overnight to a foreign country...

Not all courier companies own their own planes and trucks like FEDEX and UPS. Courier companies move mass amounts of papers and packages. Couriers are required for goods shipped on regularly scheduled flights because all overseas flights must have a passenger for any checked baggage.

When you act as an air courier you are never in danger or at risk since you generally never touch or make contact with the material you are "technically traveling with." Thus you are not responsible in case of damage during transport. The shipped goods are insured by the company that put the courier, the package and the plane seat together. These are known as the courier company.

There are courier companies, who for some specific reason (all legal) solicit the public to act as couriers for them. Representatives from the company check the goods in and pick them up at the airport or you may be expected to meet a representative from the courier company when you reach at your destination and process the paperwork together at customs. The unique details of each trip will be explained to you when you arrive at check-in on the day of departure.

Courier companies need you and since they can get

you a very cheap fare, you need them as well. In exchange for being a courier you give up the right to check in some or all of your luggage. You must either travel with only a carry-on, ship your suitcase ahead by mail, or buy what you need in thrift stores, whenever you get to where you are going. Thousands of people travel the world as couriers. The demand for air couriers has increased since the events of 9/11.

Why Companies Use Couriers:

- Unaccompanied material can be detained by customs. If a shipment is stopped by customs the recipient can be charged storage fees which can increase the cost of shipping some goods.
- A more efficient, cheaper way to ship time sensitive material.
- Certain items cannot be faxed or e-mailed such as bulky material, valuable gems, original contracts, cash payments and checks.

Tips for doing it right:

- If you know your schedule weeks or months in advance you can reserve the dates you want to.
- If you like to travel spontaneously or on short notice the prices to fly as a courier are even lower. To do so will require that you check frequently with courier companies for last-minute deals.
- If you decide to travel as an air courier on a regular basis you may want to join one of the many organization that can provide information and services for you. It is best to fly once before you join such a group. Some are better than others

and many charge a membership fee. Among the best are the International Association of Air Travel Couriers (IAATC), www.courier.org.

Remember:

- Learn the best months to travel: When the prices are lowest, when the mosquito count is low, what local issues need to be concerned (is bottled water required, are beggars a problem).
- Be aware of infectious disease issues. Are vaccinations required? Should you carry malaria tablets? Antibiotics for dysentery?

A few courier companies that have "good word of mouth" are:

- Jupiter Air, Ltd., Building #14, JFK International Airport, Jamaica, NY 11430;
  phone (718) 656-6050, fax (718) 656-7263
  www.websciences.org/dvhpub/COURIER.HTM
- Now Voyager, 74 Varick St., Suite 307, New York, NY 10013; (212) 431-1616, fax (212) 334-5243; www.nowvoyagertravel.com.

Among the many resources I researched for this chapter were the books:

- Air Courier Travel By Emily Eddins
- "The Courier Air Travel Handbook" By Mark I Field
- Air Courier Bargains: How to Travel Worldwide for Next to Nothing by Kelly Monaghan (from The Intrepid Traveler

Also research www.intrepidtraveler.com) – This site

lists the air courier companies with phone numbers, and other essential contact information including contact information, addresses, destinations the courier companies deliver to and the typical rates for flights.

$$$

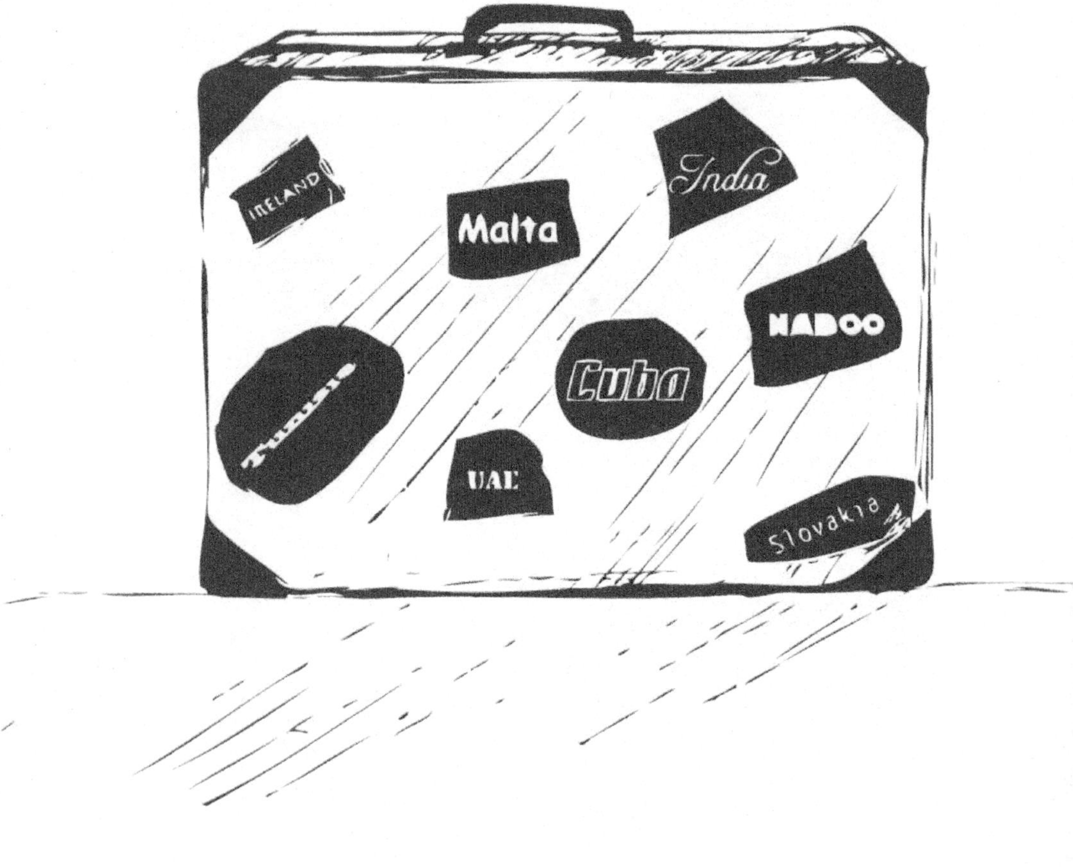
IRELAND
Malta
India
NABOO
Cuba
UAE
Slovakia

XIV: SEE THE WORLD

Save on Lodging

What is there to say about lodging that isn't obvious already? Everyone has to sleep somewhere – lie back, prop up your head, curl up, close your eyes and hopefully float off into dreamland. The question is? What is it going to cost you to do it. Wasn't it Shakespeare who said "Lodging? Let me count the ways." What is your lodging style?

Lodging styles span the range from rolling up in sleeping bag under a tarp to a high end hotel room with high end taxes, surcharges, overnight parking fees, strange service fees, $4.00 mini-bar bottles of processed tap water, and $12 daily wifi fees.

Once you figure it out the cost may range anywhere from free to thousands a night. Here are some tips for getting the best ROI (Return on Investment).

When possible stay at hotels that offer:

- a business telephone system with free local calling & voice mail
- complimentary off street parking
- complimentary high speed wireless Internet
- complimentary breakfast each morning
- no booking or utilities fees
- no housekeeping fee
- no bell hop fee
- no baggage storage fee
- no hidden charges
- no daily facilities fee

Dual book if possible. In dual booking is a little trick you can use to save cash. You book early at the lowest rate you can find. Then keep on the lookout for new lower rates by going on line. When you find them cancel out the old higher rate. Keeping the less costly reservation.

If you travel a lot think about joining:

- Homeexchange.com
- A European style residence club. They pre-sell you 24-28 weeks of lodging for a greatly reduced fee. The weeks can be used at thousands of four and five start resorts around the world but must be completely used within three years.

$$$

Pod Hotels

A new, low-cost concept in lodging is The Pod Hotel. This is a quality, sub economy property designed with a funky, mod, retro, minimalist style filled though with a post war 1950s kitschy kind of feel. These hotels for the most part meet the needs of highly social people who are 18-25 in age or attitude. Those individuals most comfortable here are those with an interest in a fun night-life with a desire to keep their lodging simple but stylish. Room prices per night may start as low as 75% less then the rack rate for a regular quality hotel room. In NYC this might mean prices starting as low as $89 in a market regularly commanding $400 or more for rooms

The lowest priced rooms in Pod Hotels may include bunk beds, complimentary WiFi service, a pair of small flat screen TVs and an iHome to plug in your MP3 player. Based on the hotel it's hit or miss whether you get your own toilet or shower or end up with a shared bathroom.

Most Pod hotels are owned by BD Hotels. They presently own 15 hotels in New York. Where a traditional hotel concierge would be expected to have access to seats in sold out Broadway shows or the most exclusive restaurants, a Pod Hotel this concierge will have listings of free or extremely inexpensive activities throughout the five boroughs and group trips for sightseeing in the day time and nightclubs in the evening hours. They may even create group table reservations at local restaurants to make social interaction easier for their guests.

Most of the guests are Internet savvy and have the opportunity to communicate with other guests from the past or in the present and future about the hotel and view You Tube showings about the activities at the hotel.

In addition to bunk-bedded rooms, Pod Hotels also offer double-bedded rooms; queen-bedded rooms; 64 single-bedded rooms with a shared bath; single-bedded rooms with a private bath; nine two-bedded rooms; and more spacious townhouse units. The townhouse units are larger, have private baths and offer more amenities, and offer more feature a living room with 25" color television, refrigerator, queen bed and sofa bed.

$$$

Hostels

These are the most basic and inexpensive of overnight accommodations for fee unless you plan on camping out. Hostel guests can rent a bed (occasionally a bunk bed) in a dormitory setting with a shared, common bathroom, kitchen, and lounge. Rooms may mix males and females or be single-sex. Increasingly hostels are offering private rooms. A main benefit of Hostels is that they are a great way to meet people from many different cultures. The majority of hostel guests are generally between the ages of 18 and 26. One of the downsides to staying in hostel dormitories is general noise from the living surroundings or from that late night guests. Then there is the snoring factor of some stranger in the next bunk with an unresolved breathing issue.

There are four different types of hostels to best fit your needs. They are:

- Longer term accommodations to specific groups such as students and nurses.
- Hostels for run by special charities and Housing Associations for the purpose of helping the homeless or individuals on bail and waiting for trial.
- Hostels that encourage outdoor activities and cultural exchange for the young. Many of these locations are members of Hostelling International (HI) a nonprofit organization that sets standards for their members so there is some minimum conformity on rules. These were originally known as youth hostels though this term is used less and less.

- Those offering short-term accommodation to backpackers and other travelers seeking cheap accommodations. These are known as unaffiliated or "Independent" hostels. These hostels are unique and diverse and may offer differing levels of service. As the name implies they are usually unaffiliated with any of the national bodies of Hostelling International or any other licensing body and do not require identification for check-in such as a passport or driving licenses as the more traditional hostels might. Some independent hostels still require occupants to do chores, may have daytime lockouts and maintain curfews but these rules are becoming less common.

Occasionally if you plan on staying for an extended period of time, a Hostel may allow you to barter your labor (swear equity) as the desk clerk for free accommodation.

Resort Travel

If you need a little more elegance in your life but don't want to spend lot's of cash to do it there are a number of options:

- Buy a discounted time share with barter credits (see the entries on barter and fractional ownership to learn more about this approach). If you know how to use e-bay effectively you can purchase time shares there at a great discount. Make sure you know what you are doing. It is easy to get ripped off through on-line auctions but if done wisely you can find great values there.
- You can get great deals at high-end destination communities if you go there just before or right after peak season. This may not work for you but if you want to hang out with the "in crowd" but if you want to have fun, avoid the overflowing crowds, and save lots of cash it is a great way to go. We ski in Utah in December – I met Tiger Woods and Richard Gere on the same day at two different ski lifts at Deer Valley. I guess they wanted to avoid the crowds as well. I had dinner at a restaurant owned by Oprah's personal Chef in Catalina Island off the California coast at the end of April, just a week before the main tourist season began. We also go to the Hamptons in New York State In mid-June or a week after labor day and fly out to Hawaii in late November. Yup, you heard right, Hawaii in November and then off to Utah to ski.
- Avoid luxury lodging: Level 2 hotels are usually fine. Generally the more you pay for a room, the more you will be charged for amenities such as parking or internet access.

In situations where you have some cash, and time is valuable, it may be best to use taxis or limousine services (which can sometimes be obtained through barter companies). It may be worth avoiding the cost of rental cars, (excessive parking fees, the time lost picking up and dropping off the car, and the time lost waiting for the valet to bring the car to the front of the hotel.)

• Renting Cars – You can get great deals on car rentals by researching online. However if you only need a car rental for a few hours look into two companies that specialize in this service. – Flexcar and Zipcar.

Become a Fractional Owner

Fractional ownership is the practice of dividing an expensive asset into percentage shares and selling those shares to individual owners. A fractional share gives an owner certain privileges, such as a number of hours, days, or weeks of using the asset, and may also offer a share of income from the asset. Typically, a company manages the asset on behalf of the owner, and owners pay fixed fees for the management in addition to variable (per-hour/per-day, etc.) fees for use. For rapidly depreciating assets, the management company may sell the asset after a fixed number of years and distribute the proceeds back to the owners (who can then register a capital loss and purchase a fraction of a new asset if they wish).

There is some debate about whether fractional ownership provides a financial advantage over renting. Some countries and regions have tax laws that provide additional benefits for owners, such as capital-loss allowances, while others might penalize ownership over renting. Usually related to travel purchasers usually own a larger share of a beach, ski, and island resort, timeshare units, a boat, a luxury home or a plane. Ownership is usually from five to 26 weeks.

The best way to own in fractional arrangement is in one where shareholder base is sufficiently large that management fees can sustain the operation and generate profit without the necessity of selling more shares.

Whether it is a sluggish economy that motivates people to consider cost saving alternatives or the basic underlying desire to own a second or vacation home, the idea of sharing ownership is catching on.

One of the most popular forms of fractional ownership are time shares.

The best way to own in fractional arrangement is in one where shareholder base is sufficiently large that management fees can sustain the operation and generate profit without the necessity of selling more shares.

We bought a time-share for cash that we rent out some years at a cash profit and transfer on other years for points that can be used to pay for hotel rooms throughout years. Since we use the hotels for business purposes the time-share maintenance fees and other fees are tax deductible

Whether it is a sluggish economy that motivates people to consider cost saving alternatives or the basic underlying desire to own a second or vacation home, the idea of sharing ownership is catching on.

Beware: When staying in a time share, fractional ownership, club residence (specific to Europe) beware of hidden or additional charges including maintenance fees, parking fees, utility fees or taxes unique to that region.

$$$

Create Low Cost Entertainment

Leisure is not an option. It is a requirement for living the good life. Your work may be your passion but no one lies on their death bed saying "I should have spent more days at the office!"

The smart millionaire takes time to "smell the roses." You don't have to fly to Monaco for the weekend and play baccaratte to have a good time. Fun can be a low cost affair and happen at any time. Entertainment is in a sense, planned fun. The key is to make it happen. Prepare! Get dressed for the occasion and do something that expands your perspective on life, introduces you to new people and ideas, fills the empty spaces in your life or puts a smile on your face – plain and simple.

There are many low cost or no cost entertainment options available and most large cities have independently published magazines and free newspapers with listings of upcoming events. Here are a few general tips:

- Barnes and Nobles book stores offer lectures, reading, discussions and book signings and musical performances at many of their stores.
- Take out books, movies and music CDs from the local library or buy your books at thrift stores
- Find free listings for classical music concerts in churches and art gallery openings
- Join your local Botanical Gardens – Call about free open houses.
- Theater, ballgames etc. Join a barter company
- Thrifty music lovers can get free theater and music concert tickets by serving as ushers. Call your local theater to find out if it needs help. Or

search the Internet, using the keywords "volunteer," "usher," plus your hometown.

- Many towns and cities offer free movies and concerts in the park. Create a picnic basket and go with friends.
- Join a gym and get and education for less: Sign up for a class at a local community college (as little as $35 a semester). Then, use your student ID to get a discount gym membership. This can save you as much $255 on the typical annual cost of a gym membership. This is a Cross Pollination Discounts
- Golf: Buy clubs, shoes, and other gear for 20 percent less than retail at www.golfdiscount.com (call 888-394-4653), says Elizabeth Cline, author of The Bargain Buyer's Guide.
- Education for small business people: Lots of free information, podcasts, how-to videos, discussion forums, event calendars are available from the government or the local chamber of commerce.
- The smarter you are, the luckier you get: Buy a low cost education by using the Video Learning Library www.videolearning.com. They stock 20,000 how-to videos, to purchase or to rent.

$$$

TO LIVE THE LIFE YOU WISH

XV: TOTAL TRANSFORMATION TO WEALTH

Visualize the Life You Wish to Live

Visualization is a form of mental sense impression. For many years wellness practitioners have used inspiration, communication and visualization skills in combination to rapidly increase individual awareness and effectiveness. By using visual imagery these practitioners have found that their students become more emotionally and physically receptive and that the benefits were recognizable almost immediately. The beneficial response to visualization techniques has been especially pronounced for individuals involved with stress management programs.

When reading articles about individuals who have made a difference in the world, you will often hear them speak of having a vision at the very beginning of their journey that made them confident of the successes to come. The evident power of visualization reinforces the concept that there is a direct relationship between the health of the body and the mind. When a person is in an emotionally and, spiritually balanced state, their life objectives and visions will be more clearly defined. With this clarity of thought and focus, the ability arises to act with greater effectiveness. This is so because with this clarity there is the knowledge that positive results are just around the corner.

Mental imagery and visualization play vital roles in all aspects of personal development both in the early creative and innovative phase and in later phases when innovation is applied through action. In the many articles and books that discuss imagery and visualization there is one fundamental point: as you think, so will you become.

Preparing Yourself For Unlimited Possibilities:

- Choose a time of day that you believe will be most creative for you.
- Write your vision down on paper.
    1. Specify it.
    2. Create various physical scenarios it might appear as.
    3. Inquire. That means putting it in the form of a question that requires more than one answer.
- At first you should work on this project alone.
- Cut off interruptions; they can stop the flow of your creative juices. This means don't answer phones, don't get snacks etc.
- True creativity does not have to make sense. Ask yourself, "In what way can this project be improved, changed, or modified, whether it seems rational, reasonable, possible, probable or sensible etc."

How to visualize:

- Choose a time of day that you believe will be most creative for you.
- Write your vision down on paper.
    1. Be specific.
    2. Create various physical scenarios.
    3. See yourself in each of these scenarios.
    4. Practice this visualization exercise in the morning and evening.

If It's Real, Pay Cash for Your Passion

When an individual lives his/her passion, he/she is boundlessly releasing his/her emotional reserve, physical energy, and spiritual sensibility. A balanced expression of personal passion enables one to express and experience the entire range of positive, strong feelings or emotions, especially those of love, joy, and focused sexual desire, all qualities that can contribute to wealth building, while balancing or controlling the negative poverty-producing qualities of power lust, rage, and mania, all qualities that can lead to scarcity. More than anything else, the person driven by passion is ready to seize the moment. He/she is fearless about asking for what he/she wants.

In order to get what you want, you often have to ask for it. Sometimes you'll get it just for asking. Other times you may need to negotiate - create value for other people in a such a way that they want to give you what you are asking for. Getting what you ask for is easier if you have information, influence, and time to spare.

Often you will ask for something but the answer will be "no". More often than not you can turn a "no" into a "yes" if you know how to create enough value and communicate that value with the appropriate person in the right way.

All of us have expectations, a personal or professional boundary; a territory that must be protected. Few individuals will want to risk their own self- interest just to fulfill another's wants or needs. In a way, there is conflict here. The conflict between the "yes" you require in order to express your passion and complete your vision and the "no" you've been given by another person. The goal is to change that "no" into a "yes", to have the other person know intellectually and feel emotionally that they can give you what you want without depriving themselves of their own expectations, wants and needs...

Wealth is your destiny!

\$\$\$

Ask for What You Want

Getting to "yes" sooner rather than later may not be as hard as it seems. When making a request for something, be concise and specific. When a request is made in this way it conveys conviction on your part and clarity of purpose. Each situation, due to the unique issues and personalities involved, will require differing communication approaches If the person you are making the request of person is willing to negotiate - has any room for flexibility in their position - it will generally show in their body language, facial expression, or tone of voice. There is a wealth of information about how every thought has a physical response. The more knowledgeable you are about these responses the more easily you can recognize signs of flexibility or doubt. Never accept an objection or rejection without exploring the possibilities for getting to yes. If you can establish a connection with the decision maker and a need is clearly defined and presented effectively, you may be able to shift the other person's position.

Remember: The foundation of a successful negotiation is ability to communicate and empathize with the unique wants and needs of a situation. Thus for many decision makers, a request made with a smile and with a positive delivery will suffice.

Requests made with a demanding tone will get you what you want from individuals who will do anything to avoid upset and conflict. However in the long run this communication style will hurt you more than it will help you.

Developing long term, mutually productive relationships with individuals who will later become decision-makers will not only give you the influence to turn "no" into "yes" but in the short run will help you succeed more often in getting what you need.

The best way to develop influence in communication is to need to listen and observe. How is the person reacting to what we say? What are the verbal, non-verbal, overt, and discreet responses that will influence how we ask for what we want?

What is the background, expertise, style, position, manner, diction, dialect, education, and knowledge of the decision maker? If you can respond to these "communicating signals," you will learn how best to connect and then communicate your need.

Though it is not always comfortable to do once your request has been rejected, asking for what you want again, in a new and different way, is a natural process. In fact, children will do it all the time for something as simple as a cookie. Getting to "yes" can be easy for some individuals but for the rest of us requires time, timing, hunger, passion and discipline. In the end the energy invested will be well worth it.

Remember:

1. The meaning of your communication is the response you get, independent of your intention.
2. There is a positive intention beneath every behavior, no matter how it might appear.
3. There is no failure, only feedback.
4. People make the best choice they believe is available to them.
5. You have the resources needed to turn a "no" into a yes".

Get Self-Actualized

If you don't know where you are going, any road will take you there. This is true both literally and figuratively. Warren Buffett's first experiences as an investor were very successful, a circumstance he attributed to his own acumen, and not to the beneficial market conditions that surrounded him. He was like a duck on a pond in a rainstorm watching itself rise on the water, not realizing that it is the rain making it rise.

Are you flying under your own power or are you just a floating duck in a rainstorm? Self-knowledge, self-awareness, humility, and an understanding of authentic peak experience are the keys to financial freedom.

To create and sustain wealth you must have clearly defined goals and visions. The psychologist Abraham Maslow states that, "Self Actualization is the intrinsic growth of what is already in the organism, or more accurately, of what the organism is."

Self-actualization implies the attainment of our basic physiological needs: safety, security, love, belongingness, and self-esteem, all qualities needed to create a life of wealth with balance.

Some simple tools for self-actualization might include:

- Keeping a private, uncensored daily journal of your feelings and thoughts.
- Read some poetry in the morning before beginning your day. This is a wonderful way to tap into your creative spirit.
- Sit quietly every morning and every evening for about ten minutes in quiet creative visualization meditation.

Expand What Satisfies You

We all like to control what goes on around us. The truth is that the person willing to pay a high enough price can have and control many things that the average person cannot. But there is a point of diminishing return. There is a point where the specificity of what you want requires a higher and higher price. The model, size, color of a car, the size and details of your home, the shape, style and type of jewels in your jewelry etc. If you can afford this type of specificity all power to you but if you are a working person, someone earning $17,000 a year or less this is not a good pattern to have. For this person the more they want that to have, the more they attempt to control, the less you can control, the more out of control they are and the higher the cost on every level. At this point the cost can put them into debt and even lead to financial and emotional bankruptcy.

The solution is to expand the range of what brings you satisfaction. Learn to be more flexible in your choices. Develop the wisdom to control that which you, leave alone that which you cannot, and develop the wisdom to know the difference between the two. In a way it is like surfing. You sit on the board and catch the wave that comes rather than expending your energy trying to make waves. You create abundance within your means. This may mean buying gifts after Christmas for the next year or taking vacations during the off-season. Don't feel discouraged. Even the wealthiest people have to place boundaries on how they expend their resources.

What is fun? What does it mean to have fun? Many words and images come to mind; feel-good recreation with no benefit other than the recreation itself, and its opposite – leisure with a purpose, amusement, sport, a vacation, enjoyable activities, playfulness, a singer, a song. viewing a great painting and painting a painting that makes you feel great, a well-crafted speech, a good tale shared with friends, fine dining, games, skiing a black diamond ski hill through powdered snow, any healthy diversion, lust in small doses, a good meditation, curling up with a cup of homemade hot chocolate and a good book on a snowy night, curling up with a loved one and a Pina Colada on a Hawaiian Beach, transformation, doing the tango, having a deep philosophical conversation with an incredibly beautiful woman and watching the perfection and intensity of her exquisite superficial beauty as she describes her recent breakthrough, is therapy, watching surfers on the North shore of Oahu, watching the tower in Pisa lean, walking along a Paris street while eating soft Brie cheese on a fresh baguette, a triathlon, fine acting in a well written play experienced in an old elegant theater, a refreshing dip in an indoor pool in the middle of the week in the middle of the week in a spa in the middle of nowhere, eating, watching the watching Condors fly over your car as you drive through Big Sur California on the Pacific Coast highway.

Fun!

Richie Notar is a managing partner in Nobu, an acclaimed sushi restaurant in NYC noted for serving the rich and famous including President Clinton. When asked the question "Is conspicuous consumption the same as having fun?" His answer was " no."

Notar's five-point plan for having fun?

1. Leave your cell phone at home.
2. Surround yourself with people you enjoy.
3. Go where you feel comfortable, not where you're

expected.

4. Go local when you can.
5. Do not network over food.

"Enough of the work already," Mr. Notar said. "Everyone is so busy trying to be the next billionaire, they'll miss it. But if you're really a success, you don't have to prove you're a success. It's like people say, 'You make the table, the table doesn't make you.'"

$$$

Give Back to the Community

What kind of legacy are you leaving behind? Wealth creates responsibility. With wealth you have greater individual responsibility for what works and what doesn't work in the world. You have a personal moral responsibility to change the way society works in order to foster greater ethical conduct. With wealth you learn that your decisions will have an impact on your neighbors, community, country and planet. Merely out of enlightened self-interest you learn financial responsibility to the world, because the more ethically and responsibly you make and spend your money, the more it affects you in a positive way. Wealth combined with wisdom teaches you that to ignore the impact of your wealth on the community at large is to create difficulties that will ultimately return to haunt you.

So the question is, how many lives are you changing, and what kind of legacy are you leaving?

One of the things often associated with the wealthy is philanthropy. Philanthropy is important to us all, whether it is the small charitable gesture of giving a dollar to a musician playing in a subway small gesture or the grand gestures associated with the great charity balls of Palm Beach and the more recent activities of Ted Turner - giving a billion dollars to the United Nations and the work of the Gates Foundation.

Charitable acts are a key element of creating wealth without cash. Why? Because when you give value - you are rewarded in multiples of that.

Never undervalue the law of cause and effect and never overvalue you understanding of the laws of the universe.

Serving others is one of the quickest paths to eliminating all unnecessary struggle from your life and creating a true sense of joy and accomplishment. By serving others who may not be able to serve themselves you are able to more specifically get in touch with your own passions and "Bliss".

There are many ways to give back to your community or the community of the world without the need to write a check.

If you have limited cash resources you can give back in many generous ways. In addition to volunteering you can also donate those things you no longer have use for to a thrift shop or someplace where it can be of value to others.

For example, we found a public library with a limited budget in an economically depressed town. I "burn" the songs I like into my computer and donate the CDs I bought at thrift stores to the library. I also give them the DVDs after I have viewed them. Best of all I was able, through my bartering skills to trade for a few thousand dollars worth of magazine subscriptions which I then donate to the library as well. This helps their budget, serves the community in a substantial way and is a tax deduction for us.

$$$

FINAL THOUGHTS

Living rich isn't enough. I want you to live rich, and struggle free. We all struggle here and there! It is part of the game of life. Everyday we are confronted by obstacles that we must initially struggle to overcome. But that doesn't mean we have to have unnecessary struggle.

In present times there is an increasing focus on the accumulation of material wealth in the form of technological gadgets and toys, the ability to purchase high priced services (spa, vacations, surgical enhancement etc.), as well as the accumulation of cash, often presented symbolically as stacks of greenbacks piled high. Despite this focus on wealth there does not seem to be a clear distinction in the mind of the ordinary consumer between money, cash, material possessions, and what constitutes a high quality of life. It's all one big "hyped image" buying immediately gratifying, disposable stuff, and buying it as soon as possible with cash. This is a waste of time, energy and most of all a waste of CASH! There is a better, easier way to live the wealthy life but before you can do it you must understand wealth, we must have dreams, visions, missions all to be achieved through exertion, conflict, strenuous and labored efforts.

We will scramble, sometimes gracefully but more often than not awkwardly against varied types of opposition. In time we learn skills that enable us to transcend these obstacles, especially concerning the accumulation of wealth and our quality of life. We learn which obstacles to avoid and which ones will automatically disappear if we have patience.

Eventually we are able to see those obstacles to our freedom that we can control and those that are beyond resolution, and which struggles are necessary and those that are unnecessary or even self-created.

In the end of the game of life, the winner isn't the one with the most toys – he/she is the one who knows how to play the game well and has the most fun.

When we think about a fish we always associate it with water. Though the water is not the same as the fish it is almost impossible to conceive of a living, healthy, functional fish separate from water. In the same way, there are certain factors that virtually define the human condition. Among these are the needs for desire, comfort, habits, relationships, love, and the need to think. This just is. Virtually every action that human beings take through every conscious or unconscious aspect of their lives, involves the quest for these elements. You can choose what you want to think about. What not think about growing rich, experiencing love, and having freedom?

$$$

If you have enjoyed this book and would like to have Lewis as your personal wealth, wellness and wisdom coach e-mail him at Lewis@TheHarrisonCenter.com If you would like to obtain valuable information plus incredible discounts on many unique and visionary products and services join the Lewis' Think and Grow Rich Club. For more information go to www.lewisthinkandgrowrich.com

$$$

RECOMMENDED BOOKS AND RESOURCES

Larry Wiener's The Black Belt Shopper's Guide! He has a lot of great ideas. Just search for him on the Internet.

Consumed: How Markets Corrupt Children, Infantilize Adults, and Swallow Citizens Whole. A book By Benjamin R. Barber. 406 pp. W. W. Norton & Company. $26.95.

Consumer Reports' ShopSmart Magazine

Simple Life Magazine

www.BetterBudgeting.com - The Free Money Saving Tips Ezine

$$$

"A poor man will walk a mile to a save a buck
and a rich one will walk nine."

Ira Hayes

$$$

ABOUT THE AUTHOR

Lewis Harrison is a respected writer, speaker and visionary thinker in a wide range of subjects relating to practical philosophy, peak performance, economics Life Coaching and human potential.

He is Past President of the New York Chapter of the National Speakers Association and was chairperson of the organizations Wellness Professional Experts group.

In 2007 Mr. Harrison completed a twelve year project resulting in creation of the The Harrison Process, a practical, ever evolving approach to self actualization peak performance in economics and lifestyle - integrating various theoretical ideas, and practical principles.

The first six sections of this book, "Live Like a Millionaire on $17,000 a Year,262" is extracted from information and ideas presented in the Harrison Process

Lewis Harrison is an "Inspired Data Machine", a powerful motivator and innovative communicator and has a warm, and compassionate style. His unique ability to obtain even hard to find information, and the ability to explain even the most difficult ideas in humorous and understandable terms has kept him in demand as a speaker and teacher for over 30 years. He is past President of the NSA-Tri-State Speakers Association, and is presently the Director of the Harrison Center for Entrepreneurship and Self Actualization in Stamford, NY. www.TheHarrisonCenter.com

Lewis recently completed Lewis Harrison's Think and Grow Rich, an online, distance learning training in the creation of wealth.

He regularly speaks internationally and creates classroom based as well as distance and online learning programs in the areas of wealth, wellness and wisdom.

$$$

Made in the USA
Monee, IL
04 November 2026

67386602R00144